Adv

Mama's World

"*Mama's World: Essays from the Inside Out* is a delicious discovery—like finding a hidden journal and peeking inside the life of a new suburban mom. The entries are truly personal, real-life stories of one mom's journey into motherhood and the daily events that shape her and her son's lives, written in a familiar voice but one with wonderful insight and humor. While the essays are filled with everyday experiences, they are rich with revelations as the author discovers self-actualization through motherhood, in spite of her doubts, worries, and insecurities. *Mama's World* will work its way into the hearts of moms everywhere and let them know that they are not alone in the challenges and joys they will discover as parents."

~ *Nancy Massotto*
Executive Director, Holistic Moms Network

"'It doesn't get any better than this,' says Tiffany Palisi on motherhood, and we at Full Time Mothers would certainly agree with her there! Tiffany has done a great job of relating her daily life, full of the joys of full-time motherhood and family. In sharing the hardships, the humor, and the wonder, we hope that readers everywhere will be led to dwell on the crucial role a mother plays in guiding her child's growing awareness of the world.

~ *Esther Peacock*
Full Time Mothers (www.fulltimemothers.org)

Mama's World

Mama's World

Essays from the Inside Out

Tiffany Palisi

Mama's World: Essays from the Inside Out

Published by Hats Off Books®
610 East Delano Street, Suite 104
Tucson, Arizona 85705 U.S.A.
www.hatsoffbooks.com

Cover design by Kristin Johnson.

International Standard Book Number: 1-58736-229-5
Library of Congress Control Number: 2004103115

To my baby boy, my booty boo, my little bear,
I will always love you.

Barn's burnt down. Now I can see the moon.

— Masahide

Birth of a Mother

I T ALL STARTED with a miscarriage. I had an "it won't happen to me" kind of mentality, but from the minute I found out I was pregnant, trouble loomed. I gave up smoking a year before I got pregnant, but was not without my vices. I drank, mostly whiskey, three nights a week and enjoyed getting a solid wash of it through my system before passing out. In the mornings, especially after a bout with Jim Beam, I brewed up some level of rocket fuel coffee and drowned myself in it until I was up and shaking. So when the little test presented the pink plus sign, I had to give up everything. Cold turkey.

I wasn't ready to make the sacrifice. I stopped drinking the eye-popping coffee cocktail and replaced it with a gentler mochaccino. I knew that I needed to put a plug in the whiskey, but I harbored a grudge against the unborn child every time I saw, or desired, a drink. Sitting with my husband in our garden apartment one hot, Friday evening, I said, "Tacos? But I can't have a beer. How can I have tacos without Corona? Why bother eating them at all?"

Thirty-nine weeks to go, I thought. Then the baby will be born and I can have my life back. That's what I thought. The little bugger would come and I could dress it in cute clothes and take lots of photos to send to friends and family. See what we made? I would teach it to say smart things so that people would wonder how I bore a child who was so darn precocious. And then the bleeding began.

I started spotting just a week after the pregnancy test gave its congratulatory sign. I hadn't even been to see my obstetrician. When I called the answering service on the Saturday of Labor Day weekend, the doctor on call said matter-of-factly, "Well, if you're miscarrying then there's nothing to be done. Just stay home, in bed, and if you don't miscarry, we'll see you on Tuesday." I couldn't believe my ears. First of all, I wasn't miscarrying. And there wasn't a chance in hell I was staying in on Labor Day weekend.

By some magic, the baby continued to live inside my body. I was still spotting and on modified bed rest, but things looked good. Weekly blood tests checked my HCG (baby hormones) levels, and I was subjected to a handful of uncomfortable internal sonograms. But there was the baby growing inside me, and I tried to focus on it.

When I finally went for my six-week checkup, the doctor did an internal exam and listened for a heartbeat. "I can't hear it, but don't you worry. It's early yet. It seems that the baby is just fine," he boasted.

"Really? But I read that..." I tried to say.

"Don't read anything, don't talk to anyone. You just let us take care of you and when the time comes, you come into the hospital, get the epidural, and let us deliver your baby."

So there it was. I needed to just live, carry the baby, and follow doctor's orders. I called my husband from my cell phone to tell him the good news. We were going to be parents. Really.

Two days later on a cool, October Saturday, I woke up with a horrible case of diarrhea. I ran to the bathroom, shocked and worried—I had to take a midterm exam in two hours. I couldn't be held up in the bathroom all morning or I'd fail the class. Surely the professor wouldn't believe I had the stomach flu. But when I looked down and saw a toilet full of blood, I knew.

"Johnny, wake up. I'm bleeding. I think I'm having a miscarriage," I said.

I called the doctor who, oddly enough, in a practice of eight, was the same doctor who had been on call that Labor Day weekend. He told me to relax, to lie down, and to wait. If I was going to miscarry at six weeks, there was nothing anyone could do to stop it.

"But I was just in and the doctor I saw said things were just fine," I pleaded.

"You just never can tell," was all he offered.

Hours passed and my condition stabilized. I was no longer running to the bathroom, and the bleeding had minimized. My mother came to support me, and my husband was home, too. He had planned to go pumpkin picking with his sister but later decided, due to the circumstances, that he should stay home. Feeling guilty for keeping him from a favorite holiday activity, I told him to go. I was okay and my mom was with me; it would be fine.

About an hour after he left, I began to miscarry. The bleeding came back with a fury. I knew what was happening and I wanted to see a doctor. I called in tears, and the doctor on call, this time a woman, said she'd meet me at the emergency room. I called my sister-in-law on her cell phone and begged her to please get Johnny home so he could bring me to the hospital.

We sped to the ER, where I sat in an empty, pale waiting room, staring at the vending machines. Who eats during an emergency? I wondered. Then, after filling out sheets and sheets of questionnaires, I was brought in for blood samples and HCG tests. The nurse couldn't get a vein. She kept complaining, "You have rolling veins. You need to tell that to people before they take your blood. Tell them to use a butterfly needle." I was embarrassed and amazed. Here I was, miscarrying my first pregnancy and she's complaining about my veins. Didn't she know that when her shift ended, this would still be my grim experience, something I had to live with? She was creating perfectly horrible strings of memories that would weave through my mind every time I thought back to this day. Why couldn't she just go easy on me?

Before the results of the blood tests, my doctor brought me into a room for a sonogram. We all sat and stared at the screen, looking for something but not sure what. Silence.

"Let's try a transvaginal sonogram, see if we see anything," my doctor said to the technician. And so they did, and they tried, and we looked. The silence weighed heavy. And then, the doctor looked at me, unsure of how to tell me the news. She was a mother herself.

"There's no heartbeat. I'm sorry."

My promise of a child was dead. I was not pregnant.

❦

During the next six months, I went into therapy to deal with my loss. It was a harrowing task, going into the little basement office to open myself up to all the hurt that had been bottled up inside me. I would force myself to tell my therapist things that I was afraid to even speak in my head. That I was unworthy. That I deserved to miscarry. That I was an alcoholic.

The healing was slow. My therapist started me on homeopathic remedies, a natural form of healing that is very gentle and safe. The remedies would not interact with other medications, they would not build up in my system, and I could not be adversely affected by them. They would, however, give me a stronger life force and enable me to deal with my feelings in a constructive way.

Before long, after the realization that I was an alcoholic, I cut out refined sugar because alcoholics often are sensitive to sugar. I was forced to eat healthier foods whenever I would get hungry. Cookies were replaced with grapes and nuts, hard candies with rice cakes, single-serving cottage cheese packs, and carrot sticks. My health was improving with my emotional well-being.

Six months following my miscarriage—a partial molar pregnancy, it turns out—we began to try again. I was in a much better position to get pregnant. I had been sober for four months, and had gotten my coffee intake to an average of one eight-ounce cup a day. We had been trying for two months and every time I'd get my period, I'd mourn. So when I got it again, I decided to bury my sorrows with a Tiffany rose bush. It was small and beautiful with promising buds, pink and waiting to bloom—I planted it in honor of the baby that wasn't coming. And then my period stopped. It stopped and didn't return. Two mornings later, I was peeing on a stick again. And when the plus sign appeared, I proceeded with caution. I told my husband and our dog, Obi, but no one else. Not until we were in the clear.

During those first few weeks, I talked casually with people about pregnancy. I kept hearing the same old stuff, the stuff I already knew, until I met a woman named Sarah. We were at my neighbor's Tupperware party, and when my neighbor introduced us, she said, "Sarah's just had a baby. Her second. Doesn't she look great?" Sarah was a tall, trim blonde with a calm disposition and a great sense of style. I couldn't believe she had just had a baby. I began prodding, asking about her pregnancy and birth, and she just kept telling me how great it all was, how easy. Hoping to follow in her footsteps, I asked her who her doctor was.

"Oh, I had a midwife. I delivered at the Birth Center in Englewood." Birth center? Midwife? I had met people who used midwives, and their experiences were good. Knowing that Sarah made the same choice only added to the intrigue. I made a mental note to get more information on midwives and then bought some Tupperware.

I stayed with my group of obstetricians until my fourth month of pregnancy, just to be on the safe side, but when I heard the familiar advice to read nothing, do nothing, and just trust the doctors to deliver my baby, I knew it was time to leave. Why didn't they want me to educate myself on giving birth? It seemed to be a very big job that involved me the whole way through. I knew that I needed to find someone who would partner with me on this whole birth experience. And so I went in search of a midwife.

When I told people that I was interviewing midwives, they were confused. It seems the whole concept conjures images of women in third-world countries, flies circling, babies torn from women crouching in huts, screaming, bodies glistening with sweat. To be fair, I wasn't so sure about midwives. What were they? How were they trained? I read and read, and as I learned, things started to fall into place. I learned of the great skill it takes to be a midwife, and that a strong medical background is required to become a certified nurse midwife. I learned that, at least in New Jersey, certified midwives must have a backup obstetrician in the event that some sort of intervention becomes necessary.

As I bought books at a local bookstore, books like *A Good Birth*, *A Safe Birth* and *Mind Over Labor*, the cashier asked me if I was going to take Bradley classes. I'd seen something about Bradley online, a type of natural birthing class for women who want to birth without drugs—the new Lamaze, I thought.

"Yeah, I think so, why? Did you?"

"Yeah, I did with my first. With my second, I just kind of reread the books but, you know, second births are easier."

"Did you have a midwife?" I asked.

"Yeah, I had my babies at Mountainside Hospital," she replied.

Okay, so there are midwives in hospitals here. Now I need to find myself the right one.

Well, it took time and I was anxious to find a midwife quickly, thanks to my ever-expanding beach ball belly. I found one nearby that I liked (and later found many, many more who were an even better fit), and she gave me numbers for nearby Bradley instructors. I signed up for the husband-coached childbirth classes and everyone thought I was nuts. Even my husband.

"This midwife thing is weird. Can't you just go to a regular baby doctor?"

It was a rough start. Once my husband started learning about natural childbirth, however, that women don't do it to be martyrs but to have the safest possible birth with the least interventions, he was on board. During the class, we learned about pregnancy and birth, but also breastfeeding and sleep options. Our instructor talked about breastfeeding on demand, which means that every time the baby cries, you offer the baby your breast. I thought it was a bit much, but whatever, it would only be six months. Six months supplementing with formula like my friends had done—no big deal. The instructor also explained that the newborn nursling needs to nurse often because the breast milk metabolizes quickly, so we might want to keep the baby in bed with us. My brother had slept in our parents' bed, so the idea wasn't novel, but still—I had bought this beautiful crib. Plus, who wants to sleep with a baby in bed?

As time passed and I continued to read, my attitude about babies in bed began to shift. I read about sudden infant death syndrome, and learned that when a baby sleeps with its parents, it is far less likely to die due to lack of body heat or a disturbed breathing pattern because any such change would wake the parent. I learned that babies can stop breathing, but if they feel a parent breathe on them, they physically remember that it is something they must do. I learned that rolling onto them is next to impossible unless a parent is using drugs or alcohol—that it is as rare as accidentally rolling out of bed. The maternal body knows exactly where the baby is and does everything to keep the baby safe. I read about the importance of holding a child, responding to its cries, and being with the child from birth, and it all made sense. After miscarrying, thus losing—in my mind—a baby, I was going to do everything I could to care for the new baby and keep him healthy as best I knew how.

※

I planned to return to work at six weeks postpartum. We needed the second income, so there wasn't a choice. My mother would watch my baby while I went and made some money.

But after the baby came and I was able to hold this darling little piece of me in my arms, I knew I couldn't leave him in someone else's care. He nursed, and I thought about all the wonderful things in the world and how none of them compared to him. I knew that I'd sacrifice anything to stay home with him. He was too precious to pass off to someone else, even my mother.

※

I didn't exactly choose these choices. They came rambling to me in pieces, a mighty force behind them that came from someplace as deep as my bones. For me, they were more than just choices; they were imperatives.

But that's not what this book is about.

My choices to breastfeed and to co-sleep are ingrained in my everyday life, so they appear in this collection of essays. I am also a mother who is at home full time. My daily work consists of wrapping my arms around a tired boy, shopping for food to fill our refrigerator, and teaching my child how to brush his teeth, how to put his spoons in the dishwasher, and other tasks of daily living. I relish every second of being a stay-at-home mother, and believe that—for the most part—life couldn't be better.

I have friends who have chosen different mothering paths and who are wonderful mothers. One went back to work after three months, stopped nursing after two, rarely co-slept, and opened my eyes to the value of mothering. I thought that seeing her with her child, with a bottle, in a crib, would have me in tears. And then I saw her talking to her baby, playing with her, and giving her heaps of attention. I realized that her choices worked for her baby, her family. She taught me that we are responsible only for raising our own children.

Most importantly, I recognized that mothering, regardless of how you do it or the choices you make while doing it, is strong, powerful work. It can be tough, but also very beautiful. Mothering is the action that turns babies into children, then into adults. The children we mother now will someday run the world. Currently, there is a woman out there mothering our future president. It's a job that should not only be respected, but also revered.

My hope is that stay-at-home mothers will someday be commended for the job we do. Under "occupations" on the census, there will an option for "Mother at Home." We will be given medical benefits and a 401(k) by the government, and our jobs will repay us not only with strong, adult children and the full heart that comes with mothering, but with a society that believes that mothering is the single most important job on the planet. We play a most vital role in the world. We give it life.

Mama at Home

YOU HEAR IT from both sides. The working mom works so she can afford a big house with a fenced-in yard, a week's vacation to Walt Disney World, and a closet full of designer clothes—and she always seems to be bothered by her at-home counterpart. "You have it good," she says. "You don't have to work." As if working is only considered work when it is accompanied by a paycheck, benefits, and a 401(k) plan.

Yet a woman's work is work regardless of how it is defined, and there are many wonderful, wise working mamas who work either because they have to pay the bills or to keep their sanity. These mamas usually don't rant on about how good stay-at-homes have it. They see the other side of it: how hard a stay-at-home mother works.

The truth is, something about being a stay-at-home makes the job seem at once both luxurious and trite. Here's a sampling from my average day. I am awakened by my son, a loving, smiling child who is immediately ready to play, and starts the day enthusiastically with, "Mama, wake up. Wake up! You wanna be Cookie Monsta and you say, 'Mama, is that wine?'" I, a woman who on a really good day needs at least three hits of the snooze button, must come to attention and snap into my best rendition of Cookie Monster, and soon. My boss doesn't like me sleeping on the job.

After Lord knows how many minutes of role-playing, I somehow manage to coerce my favorite dynamo into going downstairs for breakfast. We take each step slowly; John Henry because he's not quite three, I because I am still half asleep. Upon our safe arrival, I must open all the window shades to allow the morning sun to shine in, and also to check the weather. I will need to know the temperature as I must later dress my son accordingly. Part of the job.

Next, we march into the kitchen and decide what we'll be eating for breakfast.

"Cheerios or eggs?" I ask.

He ponders for quite some time. I begin to doze.

"Mama, why you doin' that? You can't close you eyes, Mama. I want eggs."

I head to the refrigerator for eggs and John Henry runs off. I imagine what he might be doing in the next room as I begin cracking the freckled brown shells. The house is silent. I turn on the pan, drop in a chunk of butter and watch it melt. Silence, I think, is not a good thing.

"John Henry, what are you doing?" No reply. "John Henry...John HENRY!"

Still no reply, so I run into the living room and look for him. He's nowhere to be found, and our house is small.

"John Henry!"

I begin to panic, thinking he's received a head injury or been kidnapped by aliens or something, and my heart starts to race. Frantic, I look in the only other downstairs room and see him in the corner, behind a chair.

"Go 'way, Mama. I'm makin' a poop." Oh. Okay.

Back in the kitchen, the butter has turned a horrid shade of brown. If I pour the eggs into the pan now, they'll look like they were rolled in dirt. I need to make an executive decision. Do I rinse the pan and start again or give it the old college try? I choose to use the brown buttered pan and start thinking about coffee.

I try to put my brain's brew on in silence. If I am caught making coffee, my little Emeril will want to do it for me. That means ten minutes of scooping coffee grinds into the filter, most of which will hit the floor on the way down. Which will then mean that I need to sweep it all up, and quite frankly, I'm not much in the mood to clean. I go about making coffee as quietly as a church mouse, and I get the job done while a poopy-diaper-saddled John Henry plays with his vinyl Spiderman window-sticker.

And this is just the first fifteen minutes of my day. I could go on about the energy it will take to wrangle my son from his diaper, or about the game we have to play in order to get him dressed, followed by the struggle that will ensue when he chooses not to wear his hat or coat in thirty-degree weather—but I won't. I'm too tired and the details are too cumbersome. And I wouldn't dare describe his journey to the car seat, which he doesn't want to be strapped into because, "Mama, I wanna drive!" and he will only submit if he can do the buckling himself. A ten-minute job. All this, just so that I can go to the damn grocery store and buy a cartful of organic foods, most of which will not be eaten because I am too tired to cook, and which will total well over $250 and include some various half-eaten rolls and muffins that John Henry enjoyed on his journey through the aisles.

My performance bonus for all this shopping is the honor of hauling these packages into the car while making sure that my son is safe either in his car seat or the cart, depending on where we are in our journey. Then I must get the packages and the toddler into the house and then into the refrigerator, freezer, or pantry. (The packages, not the toddler). But don't let the job description deter you.

There are many reasons why I choose to be a stay-at-home mom. With all the difficulties and struggles, without the peer support around the water cooler, coffee breaks, and daily lunches out (with other adults, that is), being a stay-at-home-mom is far and away the best job on the planet.

I wake up to a child who loves me, who will tell me that I have "stinky breaf" and still kiss me good morning. I eat breakfast with my favorite person. I watch his little hand grip the cereal-laden spoon and see the work involved in getting that spoon into his mouth without spilling milk all over the place. I see my son learning to put on his clothes, speak new words, and role-play as Spiderman. I also sit with him and color outside the lines, paint pictures for his grandmothers, and listen to what he has to say. Inside of our struggles, I see a relationship growing stronger. I see a child who once lived inside my belly stand before me. I watch him pick food out of his teeth or push his hair from his eyes and I am amazed that I have created this person.

I watched him take his first steps, heard him say his first word. I changed nearly all of his diapers (Dad helped), gave him most of his baths, and was present at every play date. I have always been his primary caregiver and I know almost every experience he has had since birth, inside and out.

I believed, from the start, that no one was better able to care for my son than I, and I made a decision from the beginning that I would commit myself to doing just that. While both my husband and I were best suited to watch John Henry—leaps and bounds better than any unattached caregiver would—I'm the one with the proper equipment. I have the hormones running through my system to promote bonding; they have been establishing themselves since I carried him in my womb. I have the breasts loaded with milk made exclusively for him. I knew when I got pregnant that I was making the choice to be a mother, and in making that choice I was also making the choice to mother my child full time. My whole life had been about me, my choices, my advancement, my equality, my time. I knew that if he were able to verbalize his choice, he would choose me over a daycare provider hands down. And I knew that it was his time.

Right now, he is mine. I am the person teaching him morals. He is learning my set of values. In less than three years another person, his kindergarten teacher, will have him for twenty-five hours a week, and that's a lot of time. She will shape the way he sees the world. He will make friends, many of whom will teach him things just by spending time with him, and I can only hope that they will be wonderful things.

So for now, I treasure my time at home. It can be difficult. There are times when I have to walk out of the room to calm down so that I don't vent my frustration— frustration at not being able to get anything done—on my child. Other times, I'll just want to sleep or read or run errands or visit with friends, but I won't be able to because my son comes first, and that can be tough. At least I remember that I made the choice to do this. I entered into this sacred rite of motherhood with the knowledge that it wouldn't always be a garden of roses, and that puts things in perspective. There's beauty in being able to look at my child whenever I please; I can talk to him, play with him, hold him. Sometimes, I just sit and watch him breathe. He may live in my house for another eighteen years, more or less, but will spend the remainder of his life living somewhere else. I will not have the luxury of eating all my meals with him or spending whole days just hanging around being bored. Someday, I will wait for his call. I will ask him when he's going to come and visit his mother.

In the grand scheme of things, these first years at home are only a speck of time. It is crucial to embrace every aspect of this time, and to document it here is my way of honoring our mother-child relationship. It is rare that we see articles in the newspaper about the amazing job a stay-at-home mother has done. We are, however, bombarded with articles commending the uncanny ability "super-women" have to juggle motherhood and a career, like for example, Kelly Ripa and Sarah Jessica Parker. And when we don't live up to this perceived "supermom" role, we are regarded as falling short. The only time a stay-at-home mother's ability is mentioned in the mass media is when something goes awry. Yet the fact remains that raising a child is the single most important job in the world.

This collection of essays embraces the small wonders of being a mother at home. It allows the wage-free, over-worked mom a space to laugh, to know that she is not the only one who realizes that cleaning the home can feel much like Sisyphus rolling that rock up the hill. And it reminds her that the payoff comes not from the small, condescending pat on the back from the occasional sappy sitcom that profiles the nuclear family at its most unfamil-iar, but from the healthy, well-adjusted child whose laugh rings clear like angelic flutter in the night air. So, if I do not see movies or go out to dinner with friends, or if I have to skip lunches out and other events that many consider luxuries, if I cannot afford the annual vacation or the big-ger house or the better car, am I really sacrificing any-thing? I think the greater sacrifice would be giving my child over to someone else, to trust them to raise him, teach him, and love him, while I did, well, anything.

Flying Lessons

M Y SON WANTS to fly. He once saw a two-minute clip from Spider-Man in which Tobey Maguire flies via a web from building to building. Whenever he saw a Spider-Man figure or drawing, he would tell me that Spider-Man flew; that was the extent of his fascination. Months passed, and God only knows how or why, he suddenly decided he wants to fly.

I am pretty good about being his play toy. I wrestle with him, let him tackle me into piles of pillows, play horsey, and let him ride on my back (using my hair as reins) without complaint. I spent many years with mostly boys as friends, so I fare well in these sorts of games. I am not, however, of the belief that I can hold him high in the air to help him pretend to fly. I have never given it a try because if I am able to do it, I will be stuck doing it all day everywhere we go.

My husband, Johnny, was eager to meet John Henry's request. While he is not much of an adventurer himself— he avoids roller coasters and bungee cords—he is very physical. He loves to skateboard and snowboard, and spent much of his time between childhood and college playing football. He loves to roughhouse and is happy to have a son to oblige. In turn, I end up having to monitor two boys at play.

John Henry can fly with his Daddy, but only on Daddy's terms. The deal is that in order for John Henry to be flown through the house, he must first say his secret flying name, Scooter McGrooter, as bequeathed to him by his Dad. Johnny's name changes to Hot Diggity Dog. After the announcement of names, John Henry gets hoisted up, his father's big hands cradling his petite ribs, and whooshed through the air. He lands, as does Spidey, first on the banister of the staircase, then on top of the kitchen counter, then up to the top of the refrigerator, head ducking down to allow for ceiling clearance. When they head into the dining room I try not to look, and then after I hear him land safely on the couch, I exhale.

The thrill is short-lived. The moment Scooter lands, I hear, "Dada, I wanna do it again. I wanna fly like Figh-da-man."

Long pause. "Okay, just one minute. Daddy needs to rest." This comes from the vicinity of the big chair we call the John Henry chair (he didn't want this new chair until we called it that, and so the name remains) while a football game blares in the background.

"No Dada, I wanna do it now."

John Henry marches into the kitchen to see me. "Mama, Dada said one minute but I wanna do it now."

Before I have a chance to respond I hear, "All right, but first tell me your name…" and Johnny is out of the chair.

"Scooter Grooter," John Henry exclaims as he begins running towards Hot Diggity Dog. And away they go.

I worry when I watch John Henry and his dad play together. They play at an energy level that is so far off the charts for me that I can't find a spot for it. I hear John Henry overrun with laughter, gleefully playing with his dad, who is always doting and more careful than most parents I know. Still, I worry. What if he drops him? What if Scooter hits his head in flight? What if Johnny trips and falls? This ungrounded fear has its roots dug in control. It's difficult to release the stronghold I have on it. I like controlling everything. I don't just mean parenting; I mean everything. When I have parties, I try to position my guests in a manner that nudges the night in the direction I desire it to go. When I cook, I must be the person to put the food on the plates to be sure that it looks the way I wish, the white potatoes gently sliding off a strip of beef and nestled beside bright green broccoli spears garnished with chipotle butter. I tried to control my labor, to stop the baby from coming in an attempt to end the uncontrollable pain without the use of drugs. (I don't like this, I had thought. I want to go home now.)

I am hopeless about controlling other peoples' minds—I try to get everyone to stop smoking, eat organic, tend their gardens, write letters in support of or against a cause, and, most importantly, to like me. Mostly it is because I have been to the other side—smoking two packs of Marlboros a day, scarfing down cheeseburgers at Burger King, ignoring issues that I should have supported, and being just plain uncontrollable. I got my first tattoo at nineteen, a plan that went dangerously awry. I had wanted a simple star on my shoulder. Just something small, something that meant something to me. But then, a guy I was dating told me I needed to get something, you know, stronger. "Don't get a star," he said. "That's cheesy. Think about something that no one else has." And so I ended up with a dragon on my back. I was always doing stupid things like that, believing that other people knew what was best for me and allowing them to point me in whatever direction they wanted me to go. Always trying to make everyone else happy, with the exception, obviously, of my clean-living, smoke-free parents. So now, now that I believe I know better, I want to show the way to others. But still, I want them to like me. It's a conundrum.

Alas, you can imagine that living with me is, on a good day, difficult. I am an undeniable control freak. So when Scooter McGrooter goes flying through the house in the arms of Hot Diggity Dog, I am forced to either freak out or to trust. I think, I am with this child all day and he does not fly. Why does he need to fly now? How is it that he can be safe and happy without me? And therein lies the issue. I cannot separate his happiness from mine. I am egomaniacal in my belief that my son needs me involved in everything he does in order to be happy. I have to stop myself and remember that the man flying him about the house is his father. I have to remember that Johnny wants John Henry to be safe and happy, just as I do.

It seems that flying lessons aren't really the problem. John Henry has readily secured ample arms to fly him on command. While he is enjoying his flight, so too is his father. They bond during experiences like this one. Perhaps someday John Henry will fondly recall those episodes that have driven me crazy. In this party of three, I'm the only one who has issues with flying. My son is beginning to uproot himself from my arms; I must open them up and allow him to spread his wings and take flight.

Wednesday

MY HUSBAND IS fast asleep and snoring long before John Henry succumbs to the pressure of the Sandman, and once both of them have finally fallen asleep beside me, it is difficult to come to the computer.

John Henry's journey to the land of Nod is a rough and tumble one. Sandwiched in between his Dada and his Mama, he carves space by doing in-place somersaults. He flips to the side, kicking my husband and me, alternately, in the head. He pulls my hair to his nearest ear and tickles it, laughing, "That tickles!" as if someone else is doing it and he is saying Uncle. After much of this flopping to and fro, there is silence. It is almost immediate.

This is my first chance to write and read since he has given up his naps. I must choose: stay in bed and read by the dim bedside light on the other side of the room, or get out of our warm bed, which is filled with cuddly people, to brave the cold plastic keys of the computer and its blaring screen. The disadvantages of reading: 1) Reading in bed requires page turning, which disturbs John Henry's sleep. Not a significant problem, but a good excuse. Since finishing the enchanting novel The Time Traveler's Wife by Audrey Niffenegger, nothing compares. Until that amazing book has faded from my memory, any other reading material will seem spoiled. I know, I've tried. 2) My Itty-

Bitty Book Light has lost its shine. I do not know if it needs a new bulb, or how one would undertake the replacement of such a thing. So until I get my fanny over to Restoration Hardware for a repair, I need to use the bedside light. This would mean getting out of bed to turn on the light (not a big deal), then straining to read, as each page will be shadowed by its other half, and finally, when I am exhausted and hardly able to keep my eyes open, I will have to get up to shut the darn thing off.

So I will write.

❧

It is November 11, 2003, the eve of my 34th birthday. For the first time in my life, my birthday does not obsess me. A shadow of this obsession must remain, because here I am writing about it, but the day doesn't feel significant this year. I am simply looking forward to tomorrow because tomorrow is Wednesday.

For John Henry and me, Wednesday is our pamper-ourselves day. In nice weather, we visit our local post office to mail packages and check the PO box. Then we walk up Main Street, hand in hand, and look at things in the windows of boutiques. We drop in at our favorite pizza place and have a slice while we look out the big windows and watch what's happening beyond the glass. We sit on the same side of the booth bench and talk about life while we eat. Sometimes his friend, Cookie Monster Puppet, joins us, and he waves to people as they walk into the pizzeria. If they wave back, I comment on their bravery, and conversation follows. It's really very amusing. We crane our necks to look past the cars lining the street to see if our friend Leigh is working at the sweet shop. If she's there, we try to get her attention and wave, calling "Leigh!

Leigh!" as if she could hear us through two panes of glass and two lanes of traffic. But hey, we laugh.

Later, after John Henry has eaten a whole slice of pizza, we walk to the deli to get a copy of The New York Times. I only buy it once a week, on Wednesday, and only for the "Dining In" section. It is my treat to myself. It takes me a whole week to read that single section, one article at a time, either while John Henry is wrapped up in an activity or playing with his Nana or Dada. Often, I clip recipes and occasionally even make them. I like reading articles by Amanda Hessner (author of Cooking For Mr. Latte), and Nigella Lawson who, sadly, only writes every other week as opposed to every week. I'll read about anything, even about foods that I don't like. It's just such a nice world to be invited into. So gourmet, so lavish—so not my life.

If the weather isn't cooperating, a leisurely walk up Main Street is less tempting. Thus, I have been modifying our Wednesday routine to include a Plan B for rainy weather. We drive to Eli's Bagels in the neighboring town of Towaco and have egg and cheese sandwiches delivered to our car. Then, while heading to our next stop, we eat. John Henry gives a play by play of how he's eating while I glance back at him in the rearview mirror. He explains how and why he separates the bagel in half: "So I eat the egg like dis! Then, I bite it like dat, and then it's sooo good!" This consumes our ride to the post office in Lake Hiawatha, another neighboring town, where our new postal friend, Michelle, works. I have chosen this location over the Main Street office because it is directly across the lot from Quick Check, a place that sells The New York Times, and so we never get too cold or too wet going from one place to the other. And Michelle, the postal clerk with the joyful smile and animated eyes, is a good person for John Henry to visit. I sit him up on her counter while we put postage on the packages and she talks to him and asks him questions. Occasionally he will respond, although most often he just answers, "Mama do it," which means that I should answer for him. For the remainder of the day, he recaps our dialogue with Michelle. It's riotously funny because Michelle cannot begin to know the degree to which she has impressed my son.

When the ritual first started, lunch was at Sergio's, a little Italian deli just a few towns over. My son and I would sit at a table in the window (we always picked a window seat) and people-watch while we ate heaping bowls of ziti with marinara sauce. The first time we did it, we did it because someone was coming to clean my house and I had to be out for the afternoon. We had run a handful of errands, including a bookstore trip, before a late lunch at Sergio's. As we ate, John Henry looked out the window, chewing and thinking. Then, he turned to me and said, "Mama, I'm havin' fun." That was that. I was hooked on our days alone, having lunch together, getting to know each other as people.

Tomorrow will end differently than most other Wednesdays. It will end with a birthday dinner at a nearby restaurant with my family. They will return to my house for cake, and John Henry will eat enough of it to keep him up until very, very late. But that's okay, we can always sleep in.

Lunch Date

I T IS 1:50 a.m.: very, very early on Friday morning or very, very late on Thursday night, depending on whether you are just waking up or just going to bed. I had promised myself a midnight bedtime, but my little pea only just fell asleep after a long hard day at the mall.

It all began when I made plans to meet my longtime friend Laura Hall and her two children, Teddy, six, and Evan, four, at the Rainforest Café in a mall halfway between my home and hers. I have known and loved Laura for nearly seventeen years, plus or minus a couple of months. She's one of those friends you might see once a year in a good year, but whose visits you relish. Laura is a bundle of joy with a big, happy bow on top. She is always laughing and smiling and is honest to a fault. She is the kind of person that you want around all day, every day of the year.

We planned lunch for one o'clock, and invited my mother, Carolyn. My mom is a fixture in our home and I take her with me whenever I can. She was excited to hear that I was meeting with Laura and looked forward to finally dining at the much-talked-up Rainforest Café. When she arrived at my home at noon on the nose, I was amazed. It is unlike her to be prompt, and because I have inherited this chronic lateness from her, I was miles away from leaving the house. I threw shoes onto John Henry's feet, grabbed a bottle of water, a single-serving box of orange juice, and a bag of pretzels, and rushed out of the house.

Five different highways lay between me and the mall. Unfamiliarity with all of these roads posed a problem. As I was yapping away about nothing with my mother, I saw the exit sign for Route 78 fast approaching. I swiftly crossed two lanes to make the exit only to find that I was heading down 78 West, not East.

Shit.

It seems that travelers on 78 West are generally not in need of exits. Six minutes at 75 mph ticked away before I saw an exit sign, and desperate to get off this Twilight Zone highway, I began to panic. What if I run out of gas? What if my car breaks down?

"Mama, my heinie hurts!" my son exclaimed.

What if my son needs to poop? Well, he did, and he doesn't like sitting in his car seat whilst pushing out a load. Fully panicked, I begged my mom to distract him. Distract him from what? Shitting? It was worth a shot. While she did her best rendition of Baby, a doll my mother takes everywhere, John Henry's alter ego, best friend, and punching bag, I prayed to God that I would reach an exit before I drove off the face of the ever-so-seemingly-flat Earth.

The exit appeared in a town called New Providence, and after an illegal U-turn, I was on the highway heading in the right direction and toward higher points in the day. Upon arriving at the entrance to the restaurant, I searched and searched and saw no sign of Laura. I was nearly thirty minutes late due to the East/West excursion and I thought she had given up on me and left. You see, I am notorious for not showing up. It is not that I don't want to arrive, it is just that the Fates have other things in mind. I make plans, get excited about them, and then things go awry. The timing of the day will be all wrong, the weather will be awful, a pile of errands will push their way to the top of an illusory to-do list. Something. And if everything is flowing along swimmingly, my vehicle will decide—as it always does before long excursions into foreign territory—to play stubborn.

Those melodious words, the ones my poor, late self needed to hear, came from my mother's mouth: "Tiffany, Laura's right there!"

Standing in a black tunic with white embroidered flowers over a pair of faded denim jeans, there was Laura, smiling and calm. Her thick brown curls fell around her face like an angel's halo. We'd made it. I walked to her and gave her a hug that was eleven-months overdue. My son, in the sling through all of this, sat quietly. I mentioned getting a table, discovered that Laura already had one, and headed into the restaurant.

"Mama! I can't wanna go in here! No, Mama, go that way." My son, pointing in the direction of the mall, was telling me he didn't want to be in the restaurant.

The Rainforest Café is a chain restaurant whose intent is to replicate a rainforest. The lights are dim, and thunder and lighting illuminates the room every twenty minutes or so. Fake gorillas, elephants, snakes, and parrots haunt the dining area. They are large and they tend to move around and make lots of noise. While I didn't expect my son, who prefers quiet above all, to embrace the idea of the place, I didn't expect him to vehemently oppose it. He tried to steer me the way a cowboy steers a horse, putting all his weight into one side of the sling, hoping it would force a turn. I was desperate to sit and relax, have something to eat, and just be for a little while.

Before a melancholy look had a chance to smack me across the face, my mother said, "John Henry, wanna come with Nana to the gift shop?" He nodded yes and within seconds they were gone.

Laura and I ordered appetizers and beverages and relaxed. This is equivalent to a day at the spa for me. I rarely get to visit with good friends. My son is reserved in the presence of other children, and oftentimes the work of getting together with friends and their children simply isn't worth the pleasure. So when I get a nugget like this one, I appreciate it.

Upon returning to the table, John Henry became apprehensive. He didn't like the two big elephants that stood at the far end of our table, swinging their trunks with masculine enthusiasm. He became tense and started to look forlorn when he noticed Laura's two boys. They were playing and talking just across from John Henry, thoroughly engrossed in whatever they were doing. In a few minutes, he went from tense to spellbound. They were bigger than he but still little people next to us grown-ups, and he wanted to look into their world. They were not trying to touch him or take his things as most of the children his age would try to do. They weren't even interested in him. This pleased him. In the end, he sat at the table with the rest of us for over an hour, content and entertained.

After lunch, we visited some (seriously expensive toy) stores and ended our day at a small dessert boutique. My son sat beside Teddy and Evan at a table that seats three. He liked being in their company.

The coup de grâce was yet to come. You see, leaving the mall after a busy day with a child who has only given up his three-hour afternoon nap one week prior is a bad idea. Add to that the fact that he was in the sling while we walked through the mall—which mellows him completely—and the following forty-five minute car ride, on the highway, in the rain, with the hypnotic swish-swish of the wipers, and the darkness caused by said rain and daylight savings time, creates the perfect recipe for sleep. And so the nap returned.

Which brings me to the cause of my late writing session. The simple addition of an hour's nap extended his energy until nearly one in the morning and it took another forty minutes for him to fall asleep, leaving me to my own undoing. I debated whether sleeping or writing was more important, but I knew that the golden opportunity for thought would dissipate with sleep and might not reemerge for some time. So now, at 2:42 a.m., after an inspiring visit with my friend and six hours of John Henry's diving, flipping, rolling, and coloring, and, in general, being the all-terrain to my son's all-terrain vehicle (read: his feet), I am overtired and incapable of imagining how in the world I will fall asleep. The thing is, in just seven hours my day will begin again. Maybe I'll try counting gorillas.

Christmas Eyes

Y MOTHER ONCE told my son that his eyes lit up like Christmas trees. "Cwismastwees?" he asked. Yes, she explained. She told him that they shone with beauty and lit up the room. Half understanding, knowing he was being complimented but not really knowing why, he smiled and returned to play.

❧

Last night, I was sitting with my son in his room. It was Black Friday, the endless Friday after Thanksgiving. The skies were gray and poured rain all day while we visited Borders Books & Music to pick up a copy of Sting's Broken Music, and we hadn't done much else. I was relaxing and trying to read, feeling a bit sorry for myself. Me, sitting in a messy house, never able to get to the bottom of the piles, wishing for long days in summer on the porch and in the backyard. I don't do well during winter. Maybe the trouble is a mild form of Seasonal Affective Disorder, but it doesn't merit prescription drugs. Vitamin D usually helps, but sometimes it doesn't.

My son, the ever-so-sensitive child, who had been trying to engage me in play with his "nightcrackas" looked at me and said, "Mama?"

I looked up at him and noticed that he was clutching as many mini-nutcrackers as he could. "Yes, baby?"

He emptied one hand of nutcrackers, put it to my face, and then did the same with the other. He looked me in the eyes, hands now cradling my temples, and said, "Awww, you eyes light up like Christmas twees. You eyes are the whole world." And then he gave me a giant, life-affirming hug that squashed all the sadness out of me.

"I love you, Mama."

And with that, he returned to play.

Sometimes it takes a pity party to make me realize everything that I have. I looked at my son, tall and lean, golden brown hair brushing his shoulders, green eyes gleaming. I thought, this is my child. When did this happen and how did I ever get so lucky? Maybe it is because my son and I are so close, or the fact that I never really leave him, and never have the chance to miss him, that I forget what a miracle he is. Usually, I just take for granted that he is a part of me because he is so ingrained in my existence. I know his every move; I know what pisses him off. It is because of this closeness that sometimes I fail to see him.

Seeing him as a separate individual, as someone who can and will leave someday, changes everything. I think about the marvel that made him—his little beginning, how he grew inside of me until he could no longer fit and then pushed his way into this world. I wonder how my husband and I created such beauty. He is the essence of joy and wonder, full of life and determination, and it is difficult to fathom that I am, in fact, his mother. This child, who has only been on the planet, in my world, for thirty-four months, is my teacher.

Unexpected Wonderfuls

As you walk, eat, and travel,
be where you are,
Otherwise you will miss
most of your life.

— *Anonymous*

MOTHERS AT HOME do not have colleagues. We do not have the professional relationship that affords coffee breaks to women in the working world, or meaningless but connected chatter at the water cooler, or even just another adult with whom to share funny anecdotes. What we do have, however, are people who enter our lives on a somewhat regular basis, who can make or break our day, depending on our luck.

I am quite lucky. When it comes to those people, I've got good ones. My neighbors are right out of a Jimmy Stewart movie, forever dropping off baked goods or dropping in for a visit. When we first moved here and my neighbor Vicki sent her husband to our door with a basket of warm, fresh-out-of-the-oven muffins, I thought it was a new-neighbor sort of thing. But as it continued, I realized it was just a really nice gesture and I wanted to respond in kind. I started leaving fresh loaves of bread and bruschet-

ta at the back entrance of their home. It's become a
favorite pastime now.

When it snows, everyone helps clear the driveways
and, if time permits, we'll all share some hot cocoa and
discuss the horrors of winter snowstorms. In summer, our
backyard neighbors talk to us over the smoke of their bar-
beques. Dan, our backyard neighbor to the left, does a version of Popeye that entertains John Henry for hours, while
his wife, Chris, and I talk about gardening. In the straight
back, Don pops his face over the fence—yes, he's tall—
which immediately reminds me of the neighbor on Home
Improvement. You can see his eyes and hear his voice but
that's about it. Sometimes his daughter, Kristin, sits on his
shoulders and tells us all about her day. She's so high she
can almost touch the trees. John Henry watches with a
slack jaw. All my neighbors know John Henry and stop to
talk to him as they walk their dogs past our home. I imagine that someday they'll be reporting to me about late
night parties he's had while I'm out for the night. At least
I hope they will.

The problem is that while nearly everyone pays attention to the relationships they have with their neighbors,
many often miss out on the exceptional people whose jobs
bring them to the doorstep. I have not taken these superb
people for granted.

I haven't always been lucky. When I moved into my
current home nearly four years ago, I was cursed with an
awful mail carrier who was as long-winded as he was
annoying. Whenever he caught me outside, I'd be stuck
with a forty-minute lament over the ills of the world, how
awful his in-laws were, and how he hated reading. But
then, as luck would have it, the guy got promoted and disappeared from my life. In the interim, we had subs on our

route, John and Jim, both of whom were very nice people and easy to talk to, and gave me a much needed break from my reality. Often, I would chat with John while walking John Henry to sleep in the sling. Our conversations lulled my son into a restful quiet and eventually he'd fall asleep. I saw photos of John's children, wife, and twin sister. In the end, however, Jim got the route and has since enjoyed the many ice cream bars and glasses of lemonade John Henry has served him.

A much-changed schedule makes it more difficult for us to catch him nowadays, but on occasion, I make him hot cocoa and leave it in a bag by the mailbox, hoping it will stay warm until he arrives. He's even been invited to our daytime parties for both Christmas and Cinco de Mayo, and he stops in as he makes his rounds, chats with my friends, and has a bite to eat.

I have also had a streak of luck with my water guy. (I'm sure his title is loftier than "water guy," but I don't know the politically correct term for the person who delivers water to my home on a monthly basis.) Anyhow, his first delivery required that he enter my home and set up the cooler. That day, two of my friends were visiting and nursing their babies when Mike walked in. Mike is a tall, beautiful man with a hefty moustache, and to his credit, he barely glanced at the bulging, milky breasts in the room. I later learned that Mike's wife had nursed all of their three children. During the monthly visits that followed, we'd talk about childrearing, family dynamics, and how we were raised. Mike is a wonderful man who has an intense fascination with the supernatural, and he can tell a story like nobody's business. I don't get to see him that often anymore, as my son sleeps until almost noon and Mike delivers sometime earlier in the day. Most mothers use their child's sleep time as a space to get things done. I use it to sleep. So whenever John Henry sleeps, so do I. Unless, of course, I'm writing.

The person I see most frequently is the UPS driver. I'm embarrassed to say that he stops at my home once a week, sometimes more. I love shopping online and often have organic food, clothing, and well, just about everything shipped to my door. He makes his drops in the late afternoon: prime time in our household. We are all running in circles, making a mess of the house and getting ready for dinner. It is also the time I am usually at the end of my maternal rope, and seeing a warm smile on the face of the gracious man who is delivering packages to my door is completely uplifting.

I love UPS.

Our last driver, Dave, was great. He delivered upwards of thirty packages to our home the winter of my son's birth. He brought them up the icy staircase onto our dark porch while we were inside, snug and warm. He hauled forty heavy packages during the two months prior to the big anniversary party for my newsletter. I rarely saw him because my son and I were usually napping when he delivered, but on the occasion that I did, I would always grab his ear. He was a father to teenage children, I discovered, and his wife hated to drive in the snow, and all sorts of other little things that helped shape who he is in my world: a dad, a husband, working to bring my things to me in a courteous and prompt manner. And then he disappeared. He left on medical leave and then was transferred to a route he'd been longing for. Later, I found out he was my mother's new driver, which thrilled me to no end, because it meant I hadn't really lost him.

While it may sound silly to be saddened by the loss of someone I really didn't know, the fact is that he was part of my daily life. We didn't share a friendship, really, so I couldn't check in to see how things were going in his life. But at the same time, I really liked him. He was there and then gone, in such a final way.

Dave was replaced by several temps, people filling in until the route was given to someone else. While these people were delivering my packages as prompt and polite as before, it just wasn't the same. There was no connection to them—no fun, because it is far better to feel connected to the people who are involved in your life, regardless of the circumstances, than to not feel anything at all.

And then came Rob. Rob, our new driver, started the whole thing off by asking my husband if he was related to Jason Palisi, my brother-in-law. To me, that was a connection, however small. It felt like home, again. Safe. He was raised in the town where I live, adding to the comfort of his presence. And then, when he'd deliver my packages to me, he would say hello and smile a heartbreaking smile that could melt ice, in spite of the fact that he has a very difficult job. He's in and out of the truck, sorting through packages and heaving them up curbs and stairs. He braves extreme weather while we enjoy air-conditioning or heat, depending on the season. He doesn't have a toilet on the truck and, for me, a day without access to a toilet is in fact a hardship. When he is not delivering, he is driving, navigating traffic, and planning his route. His job requires both critical thinking and physical strength. The fact that he is also kind to me and takes the time to be considerate and helpful is rather admirable.

Now, when I see Rob, I spend a couple of minutes talking with him. He's always in a good mood, laughs at my bad quips, and is patient with me when I decide to jabber on, and on, and on. His mother must be one amazing woman, because she has raised a fine gentleman for a son.

❧

I live in a small town. I almost always see someone I know. One of my neighbors owns the sweet shop in town; another works at the local museum; our friend Anne, whom my son calls Bambi—the name her grandkids call her—is often on her way to the hairdresser or the grocery store, cruising Main Street in her cherry red car. These people are not exactly tangled in our life, but they are a strong and important part of it. They keep me sane purely by being present, because a well-set smile on a familiar face can turn my day around. I enjoy that they see me as more than just a mother, say hello to my son, watch him make scary faces at Halloween, and ask him what Santa is going to bring him during the holiday season. They are my unexpected wonderfuls.

Window Seats at Rockingham

WHEN MY HUSBAND and I moved into our town four years ago, real estate was cheap because the center of town was somewhat vacant. When friends asked about our real estate search, we'd tell them we were looking in Boonton. Inevitably, they'd ask, "Why?"

I wanted to live in this town for a couple of reasons. First, my entire family lives in the neighboring town. I love being with my family. Second, it was affordable. The town in which I was raised sold the size of home we wanted, but for about three times the price. Third, we loved the old homes. Most are least fifty years old, and the diamond in the rough that we ended up winning was just about ninety. It had hand-blown glass windows, a nice backyard, and a detached garage. The house needed some work, but the covered porch and the neighborhood won us over. The people in town were friendly and positive, and shopped and ate in the same town in which they lived. They bumped into each other while running errands, on a regular basis.

Our town recently received a grant from the Main Street USA program, which offers services to help breathe new life into old Main Streets. Since it began, the price of homes has doubled, and the town has been written up in The New York Times and local New Jersey papers and

magazines like The Daily Record, Star-Ledger, and New
Jersey Monthly. The progress is extreme. And the best
part about it is the new coffee lounge called Rockingham.

Rockingham Coffee Lounge brings SoHo to our otherwise unassuming community. Set up in a cozy, uneven
space with a strong brick wall and large picture windows,
it is my son's favorite haunt. He calls it "Abbey's House"
after one of the two sisters who own the place, August and
Abbey. When it first opened, my son had just turned two.
I wasn't drinking coffee because I was concerned about the
caffeine entering my breast milk, and I've never liked tea,
so I didn't imagine that there was a reason we would go.
But the large couches and mismatched chairs that lined
the walls were terribly tempting, so I decided to check the
place out with my son and have a small decaf.

We walked in to see two striking women: the sisters,
both trim and beautiful, with dark hair and caramel skin
standing behind the counter, ready to serve their first day's
customers. Immediately, John Henry was smitten. I got a
latte and so did my mother (we had invited her along) and
we all three sat in some bulky chairs in the front of the
café. It was early spring and we wanted to watch people
walk past on the sidewalk. We were anxious to see who
would be coming into this breathtaking place, and who it
was that shared this sheltered treasure of a town with us.

After an hour of people-watching, we reluctantly
returned home. We were taken with Rockingham and
could not stop talking about it. We told my husband, our
neighbors, and friends to visit the place. They were surprised by our enthusiasm—to them it was just a coffeehouse. But when you are a mother at home, new independent cafés and restaurants are thrilling because they
are places to take your child for a change in routine. They
are opportunities to add dimension to our incubated

world, and to branch out and share conversation with people who we wouldn't have otherwise met.

In the past eight months since its opening, we have visited the coffee shop many, many times. We have learned, together, to like chai tea, mine skim and hot, John Henry's skim and just warm, half-full in a small cup. We have gotten to know the people who run the coffeehouse, and we like them. There are people like Mayra and Jason, soon to be getting married, a likeable couple who always make time to play with John Henry and remember exactly how we like our drinks. There's also Ashley and Jessica, both of whom are new to us, and Karen, a gifted artist and newlywed from Michigan.

Karen is John Henry's favorite. He asks me, when I offer to take him to Abbey's house for a chai, if Karen will be there. More often than not, she's not working. When he realizes this, he begins to pout and asks most secretively, "Mama, where's Kawin?" He draws pictures for Karen, impersonates her at home, and loves a song by Joan Jones because he thinks Karen sings it. (I like the song and wanted to listen to it one day so I told him it was Karen singing. Now, it's on a constant loop in our truck.) He loved her long hair; and when she cut it even shorter than John Henry's, I wondered if it would shape the feeling of adoration he harbored for her. It didn't. In fact, I believe that while her angelic appearance took him initially, her reassuring serenity, gentle hellos, and mellow presence has caused this, his first real crush.

Aside from the people who work there, John Henry has made some other friends. On a Thursday night, the eve of Halloween, I wanted desperately to get out of the house for a few minutes. I was going to Rockingham for just a few minutes to pick up a chai tea. It is literally blocks from our house and I didn't expect to be gone more that ten minutes. But John Henry wanted to come, and so he asked if he could join me. It was eight in the evening and I wasn't eager to get him pumped up on caffeine so close to bedtime, but his dreamy eyes glistened with hope and I could not say no.

When we arrived, the crowd astonished us. Usually we visit in the late afternoon—off time for coffeehouses. By and large, only a handful of people come in during our visits. This night, however, it was difficult even to find seating. And since day one, my son only wishes to sit in the window. Luckily, our seats weren't occupied and we claimed them with coats and bags before going to the counter for our order.

We asked Ashley, who worked that evening, who all the people were. There was a knitting circle of six women of varying ages, a psychic reading cards, and a local chess club playing matches. We sat in our usual seat on the fringes of the chess group. I cannot remember how it began or with whom, but eventually we struck up a conversation with a player named Joe. Joe is a man who I find difficult to describe. His age is impossible to guess. He looks as though he could be my age, maybe a bit older, but is father to two girls, the youngest of whom is in high school. Conversing with him, I learned that he once waited tables in a vegetarian restaurant in Newark, that he's married with children, that he lives in the town that I was raised in, and that he plays chess, of course. While we have since gotten to know some of the other players—most recently Wil, Nathan, and Troy—John Henry seems to enjoy the company of Joe over all.

Perhaps because he is a father or more plainly that he is just a super guy, my son, who rarely talks to people unless he knows them well, constantly plays with Joe. He will show Joe his fingers covered in playing pieces from a board game as if they are claws. He will pretend to scare Joe and Joe will respond appropriately. While he does not dote on John Henry, his radar is on and he always intuits when John Henry wants to play. Joe loves to read as much as I do, if not more, and his parenting style is similar to mine. I feel fortunate to have made friends with such a kind, smart person, thanks to the existence of a coffeehouse.

Rockingham has been our place away from life, to some degree. It does not expect anything of us and brings us people who we would never normally know. We sit in familiar chairs that belong to someone else, and watch traffic passing like a silent movie. Their chai teas are better than any other because we love the people who make them. And most importantly, we move through this space together, mama and child sharing the experience—something so simple that anyone can catch it in a glimpse as they pass Rockingham's front window.

House Skellingtons

FOR THE FIRST time, my son is old enough to understand most of what Halloween is about. While he thinks that Halloween is a feeling more than a day, which in some ways it is, this year he spent most of the days leading up to October 31st spotting Halloween. For example, we would be in the car when, all of a sudden, he would burst out with, "Mama, it's Halloween. Halloween is over dere Mama, go back." I would turn around only to discover a pumpkin, a ghost, or a skeleton with a spine-chilling smile. As the actual date neared, these spottings became more frequent, and even his language developed as the leaves changed: "Mama, look! Halloween, a punkin Mama. You see it. I want it, Mama!"

I took him pumpkin-picking on a warm afternoon. It was midday during the week, about two weeks before Halloween. When we pulled into the parking lot of the immense pumpkin patch, I was surprised to see more people than usual. Oh, shit, I thought. Kids everywhere. John Henry would rather be stuffed in a cobwebbed corner than surrounded by kids high on caramel apples and cider.

Oddly, he didn't seem to care today. He just sat there, jaw gaping, eyes filled with wonder.

"Mama, dere's so many punkins. We gonna get some?"

Pure joy.

He ran through the muddy pumpkin field—happy
even when he tripped over some rocks and landed smack
dab in a mud puddle—and his favorite part was the skeleton hanging high above his head, perched at the exit of
the picking field. Beside it stood a sign that said, "Beware,"
or "Don't Steal the Pumpkins," something kitschy that
was meant to raise the hairs on the necks of prepubescent
thrill-seekers. Its head was a giant skull and the whole
assemblage was dressed in ragged farmer's clothes that
made it look like an anorexic runway model in early '90s
grunge. John Henry loved him. He wanted to take him
home.

I asked the lady if he was for sale, knowing full well
that he wasn't but trying to ease John Henry away from
the idea.

The woman replied, "Oh, he's one of those, huh?"

One of those what? What was she talking about? It
bothered me that she lumped him, my son, into that cat-
egory, whatever it was. But on some level, she was right.

John Henry is obsessed with skeletons. It started with
his undying love of Jack Skellington, the lead stop-motion
animation creation in Tim Burton's Nightmare Before
Christmas. John Henry would belt "Jack's Lament" in the
back of a shopping cart in Target, in King's, wherever
there happened to be a cart. He would have me in stitch-
es, although he took the rendition very seriously.

After Jack, more bones followed. Wherever a cheap
skeleton was for sale, it became John Henry's "skellington." If it was not to be had, it was to be beheld. John
Henry sat with displays of skeletons and petted them, held
them, and discussed their attributes. Our house was overrun with skeletons. We owned plastic skeletons, the skeletons that hang on the door, and a neon glow-in-the-dark

skeleton. We had skeletons with flashing eyes, skeletons made out of paper, skeleton heads, skeleton masks.

So I guess it was fitting that John Henry chose to be a skeleton for Halloween.

❦

On Halloween day, we walked up and down Main Street, watching trick-or-treaters pass, peeking in at the shopkeepers who were cool enough to dress up—in general, having a Wednesday kind of day on a Friday. This was in spite of the fact that John Henry and I survived a major tantrum earlier in the day. On goosey night, the night before Halloween, he lived in his costume, saying how excited he was to wear it "a morrow"; but when Halloween came, he refused. I tried to put it on him, but he complained that it was choking him and tore it off. After a twenty minute mess of a tantrum—by me—we left the house in plain clothes.

When we got to our insurance agent's office, John Henry saw the women there dressed in feminine costumes, and wanted to go inside. We talked to them—to the pumpkin (a pregnant Mama who rounded out the costume with her little miracle), the temptress, and the butterfly, to whom he took a memorable liking. Perhaps it was the glittery wings and the deep-set eyes enhanced with sparkles; her presence sent him into another world. I commended them on their Halloween spirit and we all talked about what John Henry was to be. I told them the whole story while John Henry stood, about three feet away, occasionally glancing away from the butterfly to admire the six foot skeleton that sat in a chair in the foyer.

Minutes later there was a shrieking scream and John Henry was in my arms.

He had backed onto a mat that was rigged to scream when stepped upon, and it scared the bejesus out of him. I didn't want to laugh but couldn't control myself. The look on his face was something I'd never seen before—a cross of excitement, fear, and relief.

We were just settling down from the scream episode, ready to leave, when the temptress offered us some candy. We declined but she persisted, "Come on, just take a piece." I noticed the green hand in the bowl and asked sotto voce if it was rigged to perform another terrorizing act. She nodded yes.

I played along but warned John Henry, "The hand might be up to something, right? But it's okay because it's only pretend."

And then I reached in and the green hand grabbed mine.

We finally left the fun house and had some warm chai tea in our favorite coffeehouse, Rockingham Coffee Lounge, aka "Abbey's house." After spending some time at Abbey's, John Henry requested that we return to the insurance office. Either he wanted to decode the tricks or desensitize himself. We walked up the hill and returned, explaining to the girls who worked there that John Henry was very interested in the goings on of their office. As we were talking (thankfully John Henry was in the sling), out walked our agent, Guy Caccavale, a tall, broad man with a presence. He descended the stairs in a black cloak and a skeleton mask with bulging eyes, which completely covered his face. As he walked towards us, he was silent. John Henry buried his face in my shoulder and I covered him up, repeating that it was only Guy and that he was wearing a mask. John Henry would occasionally peek out to see if Guy was still there, which he was, and coming closer. When Guy saw that John Henry was truly frightened, he took off his mask, put his hand to John Henry's face and said, "Giovanni."

John Henry lives for this story. Everywhere we go, whenever we meet someone we know, he says, "Mama, tell about Guy." Sometimes he just makes me tell him the story again and again. Once, I was cutting corners on the telling, tired of the drama of it all, and he said, "Mama, Guy's broad, 'member?" Yes, Guy's broad.

When I tell it, his whole face lights up. It's like Christmas for him.

꽃

When John Henry was an infant, I read books on the importance of exposing children only to positive images. Light colors, sweet music. While I tried my best to follow this advice, my husband, who was never on board with this idea, decided to pop in the movie, Nightmare Before Christmas. He was just planning on showing John Henry the lovely part, where Jack slides into Christmastown and does a version of the Grinch in Whoville. I heard snippets of the song "What's This?" where Jack is amazed at his discovery of all the colored lights and smiling, elfin faces in Christmastown, and knew exactly what it was. I interrupted the DVD halfway through and demanded that it be turned off. Johnny, my husband, sat laughing and said, "Oh, all right," but John Henry panicked.

"No, Mama, no. I can't want it off." He was smitten with the skeleton in a pinstriped suit and I had learned a lesson. You can never accurately guess what your children will like, like it or not.

His adoration for Jack has extended to the movie's entire cast, save for Oogie Boogie, who John Henry refuses to look at or listen to. Somehow, he knows he's real bad. He still has skeletons lingering around his play space, the dining room, and his bedroom long after Halloween has passed. He looks for the skeletons that once adorned shop windows and asks where they've gone.

"Halloweentown," I reply. "Jack's taken them back until next year."

And while most of his mates think Barney's all that, in our house, Jack's the thing.

Snowed In

I USED TO love snow days. As a child, I always hoped that we'd be hit with a ton of snow on a Friday, allowing for a break from school and a three-day weekend, all in one. My brother and I would sit in the house, snuggled up in layers of clothes, and watch stupid movies while a fire blazed before us under the mirrored mantel in our parents Dynasty-inspired home. My mom would make us hot cocoa and top it with heaps of marshmallows, which we would try to gulp down before they melted into the warm liquid below. We would play, reorganize our rooms or mess them up, anything but shovel.

As a young adult, I liked being snowed in as long as I had good company. Oftentimes, my brother would be home from college with his longtime girlfriend, Meg, who was (and still is) like a sister to me. I'd pick up my boyfriend, who is now my husband, and a trunk full of food from Columbo's, an Italian restaurant in his town, and we'd go back to my parents' house to feast on penne with vodka sauce, tricolor salads, and more. Later, as it would get dark and too dangerous to go out driving, we'd all sit around and watch stupid movies, again, in front of the fireplace, sip some wine or beer, and have a blast. Still, we would not shovel. Somehow, we never did.

You can imagine the shock I had during my first real experience with a snow day as a parent. In the blink of an eye, I have gone from being the guest to the host. I am the person expected to make the cocoa and keep the kitchen hot with fresh soup and pasta—so I don't. I am the one who should be shoveling the driveway—and I don't. Instead, I sulk at being trapped.

My son sees the snow falling in thick clumps from the sky. "Mama, it's 'nowin'!" His glee gets me excited. I begin to tell him that snow means he can build a snowman like Frosty, he can make big snowballs to throw at trees, and that it means, soon, Santa will come and bring him toys. His excitement is contagious. And the thought of being snowed in brings a rush of joy to my spirit.

Later, after many hours of watching the snow blanket the streets with a thick down of powder, I start to wonder how the hell I am going to drive through it. I think about how it will be either my husband or me who will have to shovel through to the pavement, over and over again, until the snowfall stops. I realize that, after deciding that he will be the one to shovel, I will play the entertainer, cook, and cocoa maker. What I don't realize is that my son, who hates to wear even the thinnest of sweaters, will demand to go outside over and over, pleading to build a snowman like Frosty, just like I told him he could. His beseeching will fall on deaf ears because I am sick and unable to go outside in this weather. And so, while he watches Dada shovel the driveway from inside, I will hear his sad attempt at communicating through the window, "Dada, I wanna come outside and make a 'nowman!"

After much petitioning, I agree to let John Henry play outside while his father shovels. I explain that first he must put on the proper wardrobe so that he doesn't get bitten by the cold air. He looks down at his striped pajamas and says, "But Mama, I'm wearin' clothes." I look at this child and think, You'd make one hell of a president. I tell him that he has to wear regular clothes over his pajamas, then an overall-style snowsuit, a coat, a hat, mittens, and snow boots.

"All dat?" he questions, and waits me out.

"All that."

Silence.

"Awwwwight," he relents, and then runs to his room to get dressed.

I took a photo of John Henry in all his puffiness. He reminded me of Randy, Ralphie's little brother, from A Christmas Story. In the movie, the overprotective mother dresses her son in so many layers that he looks like the Michelin man. If you push him over, he'll either bounce or roll. Walking is a chore. This is my son in his outfit. As he lumbers to the back door, I remind him that he mustn't stay out too long, caution him to try and keep his hands dry, and tell him to take the stairs with ease. Then, I give my husband all my guidelines: they must come in as soon as John Henry's hands get wet, watch him near the ice, don't pull him too fast on his sleigh, and don't let him eat the carrots that are being used for the snowman because they're old.

I watch from the window for a few minutes, then I go outside to enjoy watching my son play in the snow. It is about as high as his waist, making walking a challenge. Every few steps he teeters over to one side. He doesn't fall very far, though, because the snow is well packed and thick, and it acts as a cushion of sorts. Within minutes, he is camped about six feet from the back steps in a big wad of clean snow, and he is stuffing his face. His cheeks are bright red in seconds—the handfuls are larger than his mouth, and the snow overflows onto his face. He eats with splendor. He is ripe with joy at his newfound provisions, forgetting completely that he's eaten it just a winter before.

Later, after he's gorged his little belly, he sits in the back of the red sleigh my dad bought him for his first Christmas, nearly two years ago. He sits up, and as my husband heaves him through the high drifts, the sleigh capsizes and off he goes. He laughs, a combination of humor and terror, and gets back on the sleigh. Again, one good pull and he's off the sleigh. This time, instead of getting back on, he's sits in the snow, resigned, and shoves a mouthful of snow in his mouth.

"John Henry, wanna get back on the sleigh?" asks Johnny, eagerly and between laughs.

He just shakes his head; a grim, "No." Done for the day.

Later, while watching children on sleighs on a cartoon, he speculates, "Mama, they on the flay and they not fallin' off. How come?"

After the boys came into the house, I was faced with a wet floor that spilled through the kitchen and, step by step, into the living room. I mopped it all up with some kitchen towels and later, when I got smart, put a bathmat inside the entrance of the door and a towel behind that. I offered cocoa, however hesitantly, because I really did not have the desire to make it, only the desire to drink it. I was trying to play the happy hausfrau, but failed miserably. There was no soup on the stove, no spaghetti in the pot. Instead, there was a $20 bill that would be paying for pizza from the only place that was open, Reservoir Tavern, around the block and over the bridge. There was no whiskey or wine for me to drink, but that, of course, was by choice. Don't get me wrong. At times, I would enjoy nothing more than to feel the warm sip of amber fluid slide

off my tongue, riding into my throat and heating my body
with a strong blast of intoxication. But then, I am reminded that being a healthy woman and a sober mother are far
more important to me than a moment of dangerous pleasure. And so I go without.

Here's what there was: a little guy, exhausted from a
day of playing in the snow, awed by the miraculous beauty of it all. He loved watching the plows pass with their
lights ablaze and flashing. He looked out the window for
another fleet of them for nearly an hour. So little with
such big dreams. Afterwards, he sat beside me on our big
John Henry chair, curled up like a puppy and leaning into
me, warm in fresh, dry clothes, telling me about all the
things he did that day. I guess snow days as an adult aren't
so bad after all.

The Christmas Fray

HOLIDAYS ARE GREAT, except when the whole world closes. For example, Hallmark holidays make me happy. Valentine's Day, Mother's Day, Memorial Day—the kind that have you out and about delivering cards and gifts, going for lunch and sharing the holiday with everyone. I like the idea of community and seeing lots of people smiling and sharing joy. But holidays like Thanksgiving and Christmas, when even the Chinese takeout place is closed, well, that's too much. It's isolating.

The pre-holiday fray is fine with me: everyone is rushing around trying to get stuff done, decorating their homes and dashing out at all hours to prepare. This is a bubbly time of year for me. I shop online and do not have to fight crowds for parking spots or wrench discounted items out of other people's claws. Instead, I carry on with my routine while hundreds of others surround me in a swirl of glorious chaos. It's cheering to be around so much intense energy.

The actual holiday, however, is far too sleepy. No one is on the roads, all the shops and restaurants are closed, and that never-ending Yule log just burns and burns on the telly all day. The seclusion is, strangely enough, the part I liked best about Christmas growing up. I knew that I wouldn't have to go anywhere or do anything except visit with my grandparents and celebrate the wholeness of the day.

As a kid, nothing beat Christmas Day. I woke up at six in the morning and rushed to my parents' room, begging them to get out of bed. "Ten minutes," they'd say, and my brother and I would sit in front of our big stack of wrapped presents and wait. We'd go back to their room after ten minutes had passed and plead, "Come on, come on, please get out of bed." Imagine the horror they felt, knowing that by 6:30 a.m., all of the anticipation and ecstasy of Christmas would dissolve and they'd have sixteen hours to wait it out until bedtime while we played with our noisy new gifts. It was a day of extended family and holiday food, Christmas music, and the Rose parade. If we were lucky and got snow, it meant all that great stuff plus dragging our parents to a hill to go sledding. For us, it was an answer to all of our Christmas prayers. For them, it was a ring in Hell that Dante had completely overlooked.

I'm hoping this year will be different. This year John Henry, who is nearly three, has started to get a clear comprehension of Christmas. He wears his Santa hat and announces, "Ho, Ho, Ho, and a bottle of rum," to anyone who'll listen. His name is sewn onto his hat, and people will often say, "Wow, John Henry, that's a nice Santa imitation," to which he responds grumpily, "I'm not John Henry, I'm Santa." Our little Santa rides in a "flay" (sleigh), whether it be a car, chair, or supermarket cart. He deepens his voice to sound like his version of Santa and talks about Rudolph and the other reindeer. He has learned that Santa brings kids toys, so now every time he sees a toy that he wants, he tells me to put it on the list for Santa. He practices doing Santa's drag and deliver routine at home. He fills a bag, any bag he can find, with things around the house and then delivers them, saying "I got sumpin' a you!" He loves role-playing and Santa makes an easy character.

I've become jaded in the past few years. I've decided that Christmas is a children's holiday. I still like to give gifts and set the house up, string the tree with lights and ornaments given to me from friends and loved ones, but when Christmas actually comes, I'm usually taking down the decorations. I just want to put it past me. Here in New Jersey, the winter days are generally bleak. There are no leaves on the trees, barely a ray of sun to brighten me up. Unless the wind chill is mellow, it's usually too cold to enjoy the outside air. Christmas decorations only maximize this reality, being, as they are, shocking bits of merriment matted against a gray landscape. I look at homes decked out in wreaths and think, "Take them down, Valentine's Day is only six weeks away." I want the clutter to return to its boxes and the snow to melt. I want spring.

Perhaps this year, Christmas Day will be more magical now that John Henry is up to the game. He will wake up to a Buzz Lightyear chair with his name personalized across the top and a new train set in the center of his bedroom floor. He will receive a Hess truck from my dad and a gazillion other toys from his grandmother, aunt, and uncles. He will see a plate of crumbs that were once cookies before Santa got to them, and maybe he will hear reindeer on the roof while he sleeps. He will see a Christmas parade on television and, later, be swamped with Christmas guests who will bestow loving hugs upon him and listen to his Santa stories.

After it's all over, I might find it in my heart to accept all the redundant shimmer that will sway through the January air. Perhaps all the lights that dangle from bare tree branches and porch beams will be welcome sights for

John Henry's Christmas eyes, and melt my heart. And just maybe all those blow-up Santas and snowmen that are on every other lawn will be welcome reminders of the Christmas that has just past.

Fuzzy Friends

MY SON HAS lots of fuzzy friends. Many of them are furry and brightly colored, and have large, animated eyes. While they cannot walk, they always seem to disappear at the most inopportune times. They love without abandon, do not protest when being colored upon or hurled across the room, and will do pretty much anything John Henry wants them to.

I like his friends. While some, like his pal, Hulk, tend to act horribly—smashing tables and throwing books around—they are counterbalanced by a more gentle bunch that includes Cookie (Monster) Puppet, Buzz Lightyear, Wonder Nouman (Woman), and Woody. These friends watch him take a bath. Not all at the same time, of course, but in rotation. They dare him to suds up his armpits, neck, and face with his Super Sensitive California Baby bath-wash, and he rises to meet the challenge. They accompany him to the grocery store and help me push the cart, grabbing fruit and water to feed to John Henry along his journey through the aisles. When he reaches for, say, a heap of Oreos, his friend will announce in disgust, "Ewww! We don't eat those GROSS things. They make you sick and make your teeth rot." John Henry, laughing at the insanity of his friend's voice, forgets that he was ever tempted.

Sometimes I get jealous of his friends. I'll be wearing Cookie Monster Puppet on my hand and I'll ask John Henry a question.

"Mama, I can't wanna tawk to you. I'm tawkin' a Cookie."

I am forced back into the moment and remember that I am Cookie, begin once again, and ask the same question I originally asked when I was Mama, to which he happily responds. I wonder, Aren't I fun?

Before bedtime, he gathers up his friends in his two arms, puppets and dolls spilling over the sides.

"Mama, I gonna bring ALL a friends to bed."

"No, John Henry. You can only bring one."

We all share a queen-sized bed, so there isn't much room for additional friends.

"Oh, awwight. I bring my nightcracka?"

"Yes, you can bring your nutcracker, but Bobo Woody needs to stay in your room."

He looks up at me, resigned but content. "Awwwright."

Bobo, as in Bobo Woody and Bobo Cookie, is a mini form of the larger original Woody and Cookie Monster, respectively. Bobo is baby to the larger Mom plush counterpart. He adapted this name from the book Hug by Jez Alborough. In this book, a baby monkey named Bobo cannot find his Mama and he is desperate for a hug from her. He searches the jungle and the more he looks and doesn't find her, the more desperate his cries become. Just before he finds her, he is in tears bellowing, "Hug!" My son is always near tears at this point, too. Then Bobo's mama appears and exclaims, "Bobo!" to which Bobo screams, "Mama!" and the pair hug. John Henry is so gleeful at the little monkey's good fortune that he lets Bobo right into his heart. And since he can't hold Bobo Monkey, he recreates him in his mini friends.

When we lose track of a member of his posse, chaos ensues.

"Where's Bobo Cookie, Mama? I wanna nuss and he says, 'Is that wine?' Get him, Mama!"

I frantically case the room only to find that Bobo Cookie's matted blue fuzz is nowhere to be found.

"Um, lemme look," I stall. I act casual as I flip the pillows over, look under the couch, scrounge through duffle bags.

"Mama, you can't find him?"

I expand my search to the kitchen and yell, "Well, I'll find him, honey." But the more I look the more bleak I feel. I check the piles in his room upstairs, our bed covers, and the hamper. No dice.

"Mama, I fink he in the car. 'member he drive on you hand to Nana house?"

"Oh yeah, let's check the car." We go out to the Chevy and search through the masses of slings (three, actually), water bottles, toy buckets, and more. No Bobo Cookie. What's a mom to do?

"Well, Bobo Cookie's not in the car. But look, I found a pen. Wanna write on paper?"

I feel like I'm giving him an old shoe in a nicely wrapped box.

"No Mama, I can't wanna pen. I want Bobo Cookie." And the search continues. Eventually, after overturning the contents of my house while cursing Sesame Street, the television, and the toy company who made Cookie, he appears. It's like he wanted to play hide and seek with us and just got tired of waiting to be found. I vow to buy a backup Bobo Cookie in the event that somehow, someday, Bobo Cookie really disappears. Of course, this will never happen, but I like to pretend that it will.

I wonder what will happen when John Henry outgrows one of his wooly packmates. Will they end up in some landfill or tag sale? Will they be abused by a sibling that currently doesn't exist? Will we remember all of the escapades that we took with these polyfil friends or will it all wash away with time? I'd like to think that they'll still exist in his heart. Maybe not even them, per se, but that part of life with his mama at the wheel, Cookie Monster on her paw.

My Son Is the
Barefoot Contessa

I ADMIT TO an obsession with the Food Network. It began as a harmless television station: one that didn't have commercials for horror movies or programs that were anything but G-rated. I could watch it with my innocent son in the room, unlike Sex in the City and Sopranos, which I had to give up for the obvious reasons. I'd discovered the station while on maternity leave during a bleak and snowy winter and have been watching it ever since. While I don't watch television that often, I will usually put it on for about an hour in the morning and then again before bed. It has made a considerable impression on my son, too.

It began with Emeril Lagasse's evening program, Emeril Live, which was the last show we would watch before turning in for the evening. The ritual developed quickly: we watched Emeril until the first commercial break, at which point John Henry would ask, "Mama, where's Emewool goin'?" I'd tell him that Emeril went to brush his teeth and that we should, too. "Awwwight," he'd concede, and off we would go to brush our teeth. At the next commercial break, it would happen again. "Mama, where's Emewool goin'?" I showed him a pair of pajamas and said, "Baby, he's putting on his PJs, just like these. You wanna put your PJs on like Emeril?" He would look at me, first with caution then excitement, and say, "Awwwight, Mama. I do like Emewool." And on went the pajamas, like magic. This continued through the commercial breaks, getting my son into a fresh diaper and whatever else needed to be done within the hour. When the show would end, I would say, "Oh, Emeril went to nurse his mama and go to sleep. You wanna nurse and sleep, too?" and before I had a chance to get the lights off, he'd be heading into our room to go to sleep, just like Emeril.

After a few nights of this, John Henry started pretending to be Emeril. If you called him John Henry while he was imagining otherwise, he would say, "I'm not Ja Henwe. I'm Emewool." He would then proceed to walk into the room like Emeril walks onto the set, arms raised high in a Praise-the-Lawd sort of way, and bark, "Hello evwe body, I'm Emewool Lagasseeee." This was humorous, thus I allowed it to continue for months; when our schedule jolted into a different direction, however, John Henry dropped Emeril from the program. He had a series of other personas, but none were chefs: Buzz Lightyear, Kristin (my hairdresser), Karen (goddess of chai tea). He continued to watch the Food Network with me, or at least absorb it while he played.

I watch various people work their magic with food, including Rachel Ray, Paula Deen, Tyler Florence, Giada DeLaurentis, Bobby Flay, Michael Chiarello, and Ina Garten, the Barefoot Contessa. Usually while I am watching these shows John Henry will color, play, or pretend to cook. He never really sits and watches. So I was shocked when, while watching John Henry pretend to fry up Goldfish at his kid-sized stove, he showed signs of having absorbed my Food Network addiction.

"Mama, you fwy this like this," he said, gently shaking the pan around as if he were browning onions, "and then you fwy it like this, and you flip it." He said this with authority—definitely in character.

I assume Emeril. "Um, excuse me Emeril. Are you making..."

"Mama. I'm not Emewool. I'm, I'm, Mama what's my name again?"

I think quickly. "Uh, Kim Possible?"

He's thinking so hard that smoke might poof out of his ears any moment.

"I'm, uh, Princess, no I'm, I'm Barefoot Contessa."

I yelped out a proud whoop. "You're the Barefoot Contessa!? You're the Barefoot Contessa!? I'm so proud of you. Ooooh! How cute. Johnny, you hear this? He's the Barefoot Contessa."

John Henry stood smiling. "Awight! Now, you fwy the fish like this..."

Pokey Dokey

MY HUSBAND'S GRANDMOTHER once said that I have a mouth like a truck driver, and let me tell you, she was speaking the truth. I like to curse. I especially enjoy saying the F-word. It has such a great sound. I love that it ends in a consonant and has a kick to it. I don't smoke, drink, eat junk, or do anything else that could be considered a vice, so cursing is all I've got.

❦

My son loves riding in the car with the window rolled down. In moderate weather, he will reach over to his right and push the electronic tab on the side of the car door, and as the window glides down, he smiles. The wind licks at his bangs and his eyelashes flutter. Usually, I enjoy the fresh air as much as he does—except, of course, when it's so hot outside that the air makes breathing a chore, or when it's so cold that every breath of wind feels like a razorblade.

John Henry is less susceptible than I, so when winter winds began to spoil his open-air freedom, he got very angry with me. He tried opening the window, twice, to no avail.

"Mama, sumpin's wrong wiff da window. It won't open." In my motherly attempt to keep the cold air out of his face, thus protecting him from getting sick, I had locked the window with my driver's side lock. I told him that it was frozen shut.

"Fwozen? Fwozen? Noooo! I can't want a window a be fwozen. I'm mad. Mad, mad, mad," spouted my almost-three-year-old, his nose scrunched up like he'd just sucked a lemon. I began to laugh, as quietly as possible, at this sweet darling whose anger was very much alive. I was laughing at the fact that a shut window in thirty-degree weather would cause such a protest.

"It's not funny, Mama," he railed, followed by a growl through his teeth, fists in the air. Hilarious.

Finally, after minutes of crying and more anger, I turned up the heat as high as it would go, and then told John Henry that there was a way he might be able to unfreeze the window. His eyes lit up in the rearview mirror and his wet lashes began to bat slowly, as though he was already imagining the chill air colliding with his warm, tear-stained face.

"How, Mama?"

I told him that he had to use a little magic. He had to say, "Hokey pokey, poopy doo." He tried once, then again, to get the words right, but he couldn't. Instead, he commanded with confused confidence, "Pokey dokey!"

His soft chin jutted toward the window as the words rolled out, making him look like a baby boss-man. The effort deserved a reward, so I opened the window (on the sly) a hair.

"Mama, it didn't work. I say pokey dokey and nuffling happened." I told him to try again and to watch the window very carefully. "Pokey dokey!" he demanded, and again I let it slide a smidge.

"See, baby bear, it worked. It only goes a little bit each time. Try again."

He continued until the window was wide open, at which point he realized that the air was too cold for him to enjoy.

"Mama, I can't want a window open. Make it close." I told him to tell the window to close, so he looked at the window, and with the same pokey dokey face, said, "Close!" And it did.

Just over a month after I gave birth to the pokey dokey game, it persists with ferocity. Just the other day, he said, "Pokey dokey," but I didn't hear him. Instead of repeating it louder, I heard him mumble, "Fuckin' window." In proud shock, I asked, "What'd you say?"

He looked up at me with a knowing smile and questioned, "Fuckin' window?"

I started laughing so hard I nearly crashed the car.

John Henry nudged toward the window and commanded, "Fuckin' window," and down it went. Not too smart, Mama.

Thankfully, "Fuckin' window" only lasted for two car rides. "Pokey dokey" is back, as long as I hear him the first time—then it's back to cursing. One night last week, we were lying in bed and he kept kicking around, and I firmly told him that he needed to either whisper or stop talking because, while he could stay up in bed for as long as he wanted, both his father and I needed to sleep. He smacked his hands down in disbelief and said, "Aw man! Mother fuck!" and at that moment I realized that it was high time I stopped cursing in front of my son.

The problem is that I think it's riotously funny to hear my child spout profanities because he can use them perfectly with no knowledge of what they mean. I always thought that there really wasn't a need for me to curb my expletives. Most people use profanity. Perhaps we don't walk around town hollering bad words—we know when cursing is inappropriate—but most of us spice up the language with the occasional shit, or whatever. I could not forbid John Henry to curse if I, or my husband, king of the F-word, were doing it. Instead, I hoped to just tell him that those words were in-the-house-only words. But if I can't stop myself from cursing at will, what made me think that my son would do a better job? When he says, "Oh shit, I dropped da juice," he hears roars of laughter. Why wouldn't he continue?

So now I am working on damage control, which doesn't mean a whole lot, but it's worth a try. When he curses, I try to give him new words, words like "dang" and "shoobie," words that mean nothing.

But then there's me, like the cartoon character Oopsie Daisy, who says, desperate to get fuck out of her vocabulary, "I can't stop saying the F-word." It's just so hard.

Life will be easier without cursing. I won't have to worry about fuck careening out of my mouth when I drop an avocado or a box of cereal at the supermarket. I won't fear being overheard during a gutter-mouth tirade while I'm sitting on my front porch after a long day of errands. Most importantly, I won't have to worry about the kindergarten teacher calling and saying, "Um, Mrs. Palisi? It seems we have a problem. Your son has got everyone in the class saying 'shit' every time something falls on the floor. Can you come in for a conference?"

Queer Eye for the
~~Soccer~~ Suburban Mom

I HATE THE label "soccer mom." First off, it is wholly incorrect for the large population of football moms and band moms, not to mention those of us who are toddler moms. In this politically correct world, let's get it straight. If we're going to be cornered by two words, let's at least do it accurately. We're suburban moms.

I wasn't always one of these women in fashion limbo, wearing clothes that get me through the day and no more. Before I got pregnant, I had some style, however unique it may have been. I wasn't what you'd call trendy; I was on the outer edge of the trend but too uncool to pass for punk. I loved wearing dark nail polish and always had a burning cigarette hanging from my lips. I wore clothes that were acceptable mainstream clothes, but with some grit thrown into the mix. I might wear a black, slim-fitting silk sweater over a BCBG ankle-length skirt but with a pair of Doc Martens, or I'd give in to a short A-line dress from Laundry, then cover it with a used men's blue suede coat lined with matted beige fuzz and a ripped sleeve, a $5 bargain from the Salvation Army. While my style may not have appealed to most, it was my distinct style, a shorthand for who I was.

Pregnancy threw me beyond the pale. Maternity jeans were at best passable. The clothes that could have passed for funky, mostly from Pea in the Pod or Liz Lange (before she had her Target line), were unaffordable. The cost of one article of clothing was comparable to an entire nine-month wardrobe at Motherwear, your basic cheapie maternity store. And add to my adorable bulging belly my grossly expanding ass, and I was a certifiable fashion-don't.

After birth, my priorities shifted. Not only was I unconcerned with style, I was huge. I chose not to concern myself with my appearance, to focus more on mothering my child, clearly the more pressing responsibility. I had to figure out how to nurse, which took about three months to achieve proficiency, and then how to get my restless baby to fall asleep in my arms or in our sling. I had to figure out how to brush my teeth in the morning, cook or warm food, and on occasion, shower. The possibility of getting up and putting on makeup, squeezing into some decent clothes, and doing my hair didn't enter my mind. Functioning on intermittent sleep was enough to keep me busy around the clock.

After endless months in torn jeans, T-shirts for extra-large men, and Birkenstocks, my husband voiced concern. He'd known me for over seven years, and never during the course of that time had I been so unkempt. My hair, which was once consistently shoulder length and Ultra Light Golden Blonde, had become a long, undyed, graying mass. My brows had grown into small caterpillars keeping watch over my eyes. Any sense of self-care had been banished in place of delirious mama love. It was frightening. What next? Unshaven legs?

I decided that it was high time to do something. But I couldn't go back to the old pre-pregnancy clothes. For one, they were not practical. What mother of a toddler tromps around in three-inch strappy heels, $200 skirts, and dry-clean-only tops? The shoes would fetter my ability to chase John Henry. Skirts, in general, are not practical for a mom who spends her time bending, cleaning, and running errands with a toddler. And what about that nice, dry-clean-only shirt? Imagine.

I afflicted myself with the only solution I saw fit. I would become, horror of horrors, a soccer mom. Just admitting it gave me the creeps. First, I attempted to create the look on my own. I picked up some white canvas Tommy Hilfiger sneakers, and then went to various shops in search of cute drawstring Capri pants with solid cotton/poly tees to match. It all seemed okay until it was on my body. I looked at myself and saw something awful. It was like those movies where an old person swaps bodies with a kid and the clothes don't match the body it dresses. In fact, it was so bad that I believe I would have been able to obtain a senior discount at Sizzler without being carded. I tried to upgrade the whole thing with a trip to Ann Taylor. While this improved the look and quality of the apparel, it just wasn't me.

After making some dumpster divers very happy, I started anew. Fuck it, I thought. I'm going to wear what I feel like wearing. I picked up a bunch of Gap low riders to hug my hips in just the right places, then I ripped through the Urban Outfitters catalog in search of tiny tees. I bought a bunch in a size large (the largest size available), in part to accommodate my generous rack and in part because I know that they are sized to fit women like Giselle Bundchen, or my sister-in-law, who has not had a child and can wear nearly anything without worry. So when my "Everyone Loves an Italian Girl" tee came in the mail, I felt like a born-again hipster.

And then I tried it on. The cute jeans that hugged just low enough to offer a peek of panties—they were awful. Instead of looking like a casually dressed Paris Hilton, I looked like a Sumo wrestler with plumber's crack. I spent half my day trying to keep them up high enough to hide my heinie and the other half trying to pull the mini shirt down and over the waistline. Instead of showing a slip of skin, the whole right side of it would race up to my bra line every time I hoisted my toddler onto my hip, displaying a large love handle that no one wanted to hold on to.

After many desperate battles against motherhood's grip on my closet, I am back to my desperately boring, stay-at-home mama wardrobe: jeans that fit with some room to spare, long sleeve cotton tees with crew necks, and ten-year-old, scuffed, perfectly worn-in Angels by John Fluevog.

I wonder what Queer Eye's Fab 5 would do to me, with me. I fantasize that hunky Kyan, the beauty expert, would take me to a salon, have my hair cut in a shoulder length blunt cut tripped-up with white highlights. I imagine that he would get me a facial and some properly plucked eyebrows from Bliss's Marcia Kilgore. While I am away, being beautified with my son in my arms the whole time (because I'd never, ever leave him for so long) Thom the decorator would repaint the shell of a room we call a home office with a delicate earth tone, build bookshelves into the wall, buy me a new mahogany desk from Ethan Allen with a gorgeous leather desk chair, and stuff a big, cozy reading chair into the corner. Carson the fashionista would take me to the hippest little boutiques in Chelsea and SoHo, lavish attention upon me, and find me cool, comfortable clothes to fill my modest closet. Chef Ted would teach me how to make some ridiculously wonderful meal, something Italian and very cheesy, but naturally fat-free and, of course, all organic. And Jai, well, he'd have to teach me how to live in the world as a mommy and a woman, both at the same time.

Busted

I THINK I will be going bra shopping sometime soon. It's been so long—three years, really—and I want nothing more than to push my breasts into some glorious lacy underwire bras whose straps actually look sexy when they peek out of a shirt.

My breasts—hooters, boulders, milk wagons, boobs, coconuts, knockers—have functioned as only one thing since early 2001: Nursey Babies. I have been lactating since the sixth month of my pregnancy and, finally, I am ready to quit my job at the dairy factory. I didn't believe that I would ever be happy at the prospect of my son giving up nursing. I'd look at him, and then at my mother, and ask, "Mom, how will I be when he stops nursing? I think I'll die." I loved his milky smile and the way the breast milk put him into a kind of blissful trance.

Now, as he is slowly traveling the route to pasteurized dairy only, I am ready. I still love the milky smile, but it works just as well with Organic Valley Whole Milk. I don't wish to rush him from my breasts but, at the same time, I am grateful that he is outgrowing it.

The last time I attempted an essay about breastfeeding, and about how my son was weaning, he started nursing every three hours the very next day. The goddesses of lingerie, it seemed, were heckling me. I feel confident as I write this, though, because over the past two weeks my son has only nursed when he first woke up in the mornings and, on occasion, during the night. Today, for example, he only nursed once, right when he woke up.

I hadn't expected to be nursing a toddler. Prior to my son's birth, I thought I'd nurse for six months. After he was born, I upped it to a year. Now, just two months before he turns three, I think about how naïve I had been. Who imagines the benefits of nursing an older child—for instance, the ability to reconnect over a comforting breast after a tantrum, or the amazing ability it has to keep a sick child from dehydrating. I will miss this part of breastfeeding so very much.

But then I think about having my breasts back. I fantasize about burning all the raggedy, worn nursing bras and lifting (heaving) my rack into a form-fitting push-up from Victoria's Secret. The fact that I will need to push up my breasts just to keep from having to tuck them into the waist of my pants only adds to the need for new bras. Perhaps a Wonderbra would be more suitable. Or maybe there is an actual bra for women who have been to the other side and then have returned, slack and droopy. I think that's what we need, a line of bras for women who've done it all and wish to return to a shadow of their former selves. I used to have 38Cs and, while they were far from perky, they in no way resemble the globes that now grace my chest. They need to be lifted front and center, so bra-strap durability is required. Not to mention padding that reshapes the orbs that remain.

I'm exaggerating. Those who know me know that I am not that kind of girl. I am a practical, form-before-function kind of girl, and I believe that the true value of a breast lies in its ability to nourish a child. But wouldn't it be nice, just for a minute, to have breasts that look as voluptuous and amazing as they truly are?

Vertigo

I DON'T USUALLY get sick. I get colds and things, but never anything memorable. On the rare occasions that something like stomach pains or other stinging feelings strike, I worry that I am dying.

When I woke up after a short snooze that resulted from putting my son to bed (fake it 'til you make it really works) just before midnight, I sat up with the intention of leaving the bed to send e-mails and surf the net. As I began to rise, my head went hurtling back towards the bed. I picked it up again and felt the same sensation. I was half asleep so I just chalked it up to being really, really tired and gave in to the pillow's softness.

I'd had a rough afternoon. After visiting a favorite local shop, I was preparing to walk out with over $100 worth of Christmas booty—Day of the Dead sculptures. Before leaving, I noticed a beautiful journal with dancing skeletons on the cover. It looked to be decoupaged and, having had my interest piqued, I decided to pull it from the shelf for a closer look. While trying to figure out how it was made, the owner of the store showed me a similar, smaller journal. I asked her about the one that I held in my hand and she told me about the artist who bound the books. I put the book back, all while the store owner looked on, and as I placed it on the shelf, I heard a tinny tink. In putting back the journal, I'd tapped the arm of a delicate statue that was right next to it (frankly a stupid place to put a journal, in such close proximity to a break-able statue) and knocked it off. And lucky me, I got to take the broken betty home for a bargain price of $245. (The statue, at the time of this writing, sits in my attic in need of some gluing and, if I ever get around to it, I will bring it to the local Mexican restaurant to see if they'd like to give her a home.)

I was sick about this. I really am not in a position to drop $245 on an ugly broken statue. I'd hoped that the shop owner, who knew me and knew that I frequently dropped some serious cash in the place, would be savvy enough to tell me to forget about it. No such luck. So she lost a customer and I gained a steep incline of debt.

I'd worried about it for the entire evening and, after having gone to bed that night, I could think only of this horrific incident. I wondered what others might have done if they'd been in my position, or if they hadn't had that kind of money or a credit card. I was haunted by the fact that I am still a girl trying to please the world. I want to be liked at all costs, even by the woman who was stick-ing it to me for two hundred-plus dollars. I wondered why I'd ever gone into that store anyway, despite the fact that it was damn cold that Sunday afternoon and I really need-ed to get to my mother's house. I later remembered that I visited the store because I wanted to throw a little business their way during the holiday season. Stupid. And what a lesson it was.

I woke up about two hours later, just before 2 a.m., for something—whether it was to roll over or go to the bath-room, I don't know—and felt lost in space. Every time I tried to change the direction I was looking in, the rest of the room would follow in a slow swoosh. The back of my head felt like it was capped with a forty-pound skull harness. If I even thought about sitting up, I'd start to fall. I panicked.

I woke my husband from sleep to tell him, "Johnny, something's wrong. Really wrong. With me."

He peeked over at me, sitting at attention in an attempt to feign alertness at such an early hour. I tried to explain that the room wasn't steady, that I couldn't find my center, but it's hard to find the words to explain vertigo. And while I think I may have said, "I have vertigo," he just didn't get it.

"Put your foot on the floor, it will stop the spinning," he advised.

"Look, it's not like when you get bed spins while your drunk, it's like, I can't walk. Come here and help me." I got up with Johnny's assistance and walked to the bathroom. I don't know why I wanted to be in the bathroom. Maybe I felt I needed to talk to Johnny without fear of waking up my son, who slept in our bed. Or maybe I believed the bathroom would make things more clear. The clean, white tiles of the floor seemed somehow to right the moment. If I focused on them, everything would be fine. Breathing, however, caused movement and I began to feel really bad. Perhaps I needed to vomit (something I haven't done in over fifteen years), or worse, I was dying.

Brain aneurysm, I thought. It's something I've feared since the first time I heard about it. An old coworker named Ron had lost his thirty-year-old brother-in-law to a brain aneurysm. No warning signs, no symptoms. He just died. Then I thought that the vertigo was part of a heart attack. Don't ask me why, it just seemed like a possibility. The minute I thought it might have been a heart attack, I made a mental note of all the cheese that I eat and thought, "Well, here you go. Here's your reward." I also thought that I might pass out. I asked my husband to bring me the cordless phone and I called my mom. She has the ability to realign the planets, in my eyes. She is still up high on a pedestal—something she's been trying to jump from for some time now, being sick of the responsibility it passes to her—and I always feel safer when I hear her voice.

When she answered, I could tell she was frightened that the person on the other line had awful news to share. The phone usually doesn't ring at 2 a.m. with good news. Both of her parents have rocky health records—her dad has chronic lymphocytic leukemia and her mom was recently released from the hospital with oxygen. So I knew that when she answered and heard my voice, she'd think it was John Henry.

"Mom, it's me. Something's wrong, really wrong, with me. I have vertigo. Do you think I'm dying?" all in one breath.

"Vertigo? No, Tiffany. I don't think you're dying," she replied with a hint of sarcasm. My mother thinks I'm a drama queen, so she never takes anything I say, when it comes to my health concerns, to heart. "Susan gets that a lot. I think Christie does, too."

Whew. Not alone. But still what could be the cause? Why me? Why now? My mother started listing homeopathic remedies I could take to help the vertigo. I wrote them down while sending Johnny for my bag of remedies (the one that's always missing), and then I hung up with my mom and wondered what to do next. The thought of going to the emergency room occurred to me. It was such a strong thought that I actually told my husband to get dressed and asked him how we were going to get the baby dressed and to the car. He'd be so cranky. I said, "I might be dying but then, if I'm not, will the trip be worth all the aggravation?"

Johnny replied, "Will he be better off if you're dead? Let's go."

While he was gathering his clothes, I thought about the protocol for ER. Usually, they like to watch their patients, do tests to rule things out, and various other things that would cause my son and me to be separated for hours on end. This would be horrific. I never leave my son—the trauma of being separated, really separated, for the first time in a hospital of all places, would be gruesome. I think that if I truly believed that I was dying I would definitely have gone to the ER. However, something told me that calling the doctor would serve me better.

I called the doctor's office. My new family doctor is a wonderful DO who listens, listens, listens, without interrupting. She doesn't presume to know it all when the reality is that she knows more than most of the doctors I've met. She is relatively new to our family, though, and I could not remember her office's telephone number. The number I was able to recall was of my old doctor, a big practice that likes giving out antibiotics for everything. While I did not want to be misdiagnosed or wrongly medicated, I did want to know that I was going to survive the night.

Desperate, I called my former practice. About five minutes later, maybe less, the doctor on call was ringing my line. When he identified himself, I remembered that he is not part of the practice but is an independent doctor. I asked him if he'd joined the practice and he explained that he hadn't, just that he'd occasionally cover for them. I explained what was going on, telling him that I'd also taken 1000 mg of Ester C, 1000 IUs of Vitamin D, and a shelf stable acidophilus before going to bed. He told me that he wasn't concerned about the vitamins before bed and believed that the cause of my vertigo was fluid collecting in my inner ear. He said that he was confident that I was not dying, nor in need of an ER visit, and that I should see my doctor in the morning. At that moment, and still now, he is an angel.

When I was able to get an appointment with my doctor the following morning, my mom offered to come and help with my son. My husband started the car and helped me pack John Henry into his big, stuffy winter coat, explaining that mama was sick and he needed to help her.

"Mama's sick? Oh, awwight."

We told him that Mama was going to see Dr. Naper (not her name, but the name that John Henry has bestowed on her) and that only mama was going to be looked at, not John Henry.

"Oh, awwight."

We told him that, when he got to the two story building, he could ride the elevator. "Like on a'cation?" he asked.

"Yes, baby. Like on vacation."

He looked at me, confused and thrilled both at the same time. "Awwwight."

It turns out that the doctor on call hit the nail on the head. Somehow I'd contracted a head cold without knowing it, and the mucus had backed up into my inner ear. Fortunately, it was diagnosed as viral, which meant no antibiotics. This was good because I hate antibiotics. They wreak havoc on your system and usually cause as much trouble as they are meant to relieve. I was sent home with a prescription for Antivert, to help manage my symptoms until they'd passed.

For the remainder of that day, and again the following day, my mom, who is forever the germophobe, stayed at my house to play with my son and help take care of him until my husband came home. By the third day, Wednesday, I felt that I was able to drive, and I really needed to get out and get some help. My mother had a Qi-Gong appointment that day at her house, and the only way I'd get a break, some help, and a change of scenery, was to go to her house.

It wasn't until about ten minutes into the normally six-minute ride that I realized I shouldn't have been driving. I felt like I was driving drunk. To keep from driving into a ditch, I focused hard on the road. My head hurt from focusing. My eyes stung and I wondered if I was closer to my mom's house or to mine. I decided, God knows how, that I was closer to her house than to mine, and so I proceeded. From the backseat came a little voice: "Mama, I want Cookie Monsta a dwive." The thought of Cookie Monster, and if I even had him, was too much.

"John Henry, Mama can't see and her head is really sick so you have to wait for Cookie 'til we get to Nana's. Okay?"

"No Mama, I can't wanna wait. I want Cookie Monsta, he says, 'Move it ovah sista,' awwight?"

Normally, Cookie Monster steers on the right hand and yells things at cars like, "Move it ovah, sista!" or, "Lady, hey lady. Giva guya break, heah!" From the start, Cookie Monster has spoken Brooklynease. It sounds hellish to the innocent bystander or to the gentle mom with the little baby nursing at her breast. I want to say, "You'll do it, too. Just you wait." But I know that I may be wrong, and so I keep my trap shut.

Driving was stupid. I had my precious, innocent little guy strapped into his Fisher-Price seat, but does that make

him safe? I, driving twenty miles per hour down main
roads, braking to round a turn, was plain dumb. In retro-
spect, I wouldn't do it again. (Maybe there is a slight
chance, since I know it all turned out well in the end.) I
no longer have only myself to think about; there is my son,
my child. He trusts me. He believes that I will always do
my best to protect him. This was a time that I threw caution to the wind and I could have failed him.

Today, four days later, I was finally able to drive without fear or threat of injuring someone. I visited the post
office first, having to get John Henry bundled into three
unwanted layers and then into the sling. It was dreadful.
He smacked his head on the back of the passenger's front
seat when popping out of his mini one (the seat had been
pushed back from my trip to the doctor), then he got into
my sling in tears, loaded in layers of clothing. Finally, I
had to lug about five pounds of newsletters to the counter, box (build the box to send them in, too), and address
them. By the time I got to the postal clerk I wondered if I
was going to pass out. But as soon as I'd returned to the
car, gotten John Henry back into his seat, and returned to
the driver's side, I knew I was going to be okay. Add to
that the great smile and excited wave I got from a friend
driving by on Main Street, and the day was bright.

Later, while shopping at my favorite grocery store, I
told one of the people who works there all about my experience, and he said that he often gets vertigo on elevators.
We began taking about it and he explained that vertigo is
a condition that is often brought on by a serious amount
of stress. Having been as stressed as I probably could have
been, given the $245 mistake of the day, I believe I know
what brought it on. I am very sensitive and can easily be
bothered by traumatic situations. While I cannot wholly
blame the nasty blonde, who put all loveliness aside when

I asked her to please find it in her heart to allow me to return the statue for cash, to which she replied in her best Jersey accent, "Uhight (short for alright), I see where you're comin' from but we need to make money, and I'm willin' ta meet ya halfway and charge you what I paid..." for my post-traumatic stress attack, I sure believe that the dreadful incident in her store triggered it.

Regardless of the cause, this experience has given my son the opportunity to grow. He has learned that his mother can need his help and that he can respond in kind. Every time I'd smile, he'd ask, "You all betta Mama?" and when I'd answer, "No," he'd mask his sadness with a hard-working smile, and say, "Awwight, you gonna be betta soon." He tested my strength, at times, challenging me by doing things he knows he shouldn't do, just because he saw I was lying down and not as quick to follow through on my, "No." It taught me how to explain the reasons behind the "No," like why he shouldn't climb on the counter or lie on the stairs. Mostly, though, it reminded me that life is more about how we perceive things than how they actually are.

Misfit Mama

W HAT'S THE DEAL with all the new mom clubs popping up in every corner of the country? I understand that mothers at home can, at times, feel isolated and that it's good to have company—but these paying-dues type of groups? They are so organized and formal. I guess it's good to know that there is someone in charge, a ringleader of sorts, someone to make sure everybody knows the sick policy, someone to book the rooms for special events, but somehow, it reminds me of high school. Like the girls in the club are the popular ones who sneak out of the house and date all the really cute boys, and I am, once again, the outsider.

I am not opposed to the idea of groups for women, groups that support a mother's work. After my son's birth, I initiated a moms' group of sorts, comprised of mothers who share parenting practices. We took turns meeting at each others' homes in the mornings and, while there, we'd discuss things that carried meaning for us. We'd talk about vaccinations, breastfeeding, co-sleeping, and gentle discipline.

Nowadays, my son and I and wake up very late in the morning, but the group still continues without us. We no longer attend groups that we loved, like La Leche League, for the same reason. My dear friend Nancy is the executive director of a wonderful group, Holistic Moms Network, that meets monthly, invites children, and usually has a speaker. While the moms in this group have children of varying ages, they all share one common thread: they live holistically. These are the mom groups that I love.

The mom groups that I don't feel I can mesh with, though, are these I'm-a-mom-you're-a-mom-let's-socialize kinds. They are made up of mothers who need and want support while they are at home. While I can see why someone might be drawn to this type of club (I was; I joined one), I have found that they are far different from what I'd expected.

The mom group that I joined just a month ago sends out a calendar with a list of events. These events include a weekly playgroup and several other social opportunities. Most of the events that I'd like to attend happen early in the morning. I realize that most children are up at the first call of the rooster and our 11 a.m. roll out of bed is not, well, normal, but it does pose a problem when it comes to actually meeting someone from the club. They have a coffee and crayons group that meets at Rockingham, my favorite coffee lounge, at ten in the morning. Ouch. Much too early. I can, however, make the lunch dates that fall somewhere around noon. Forget that we'll be ordering our eggs over easy while the remainder of the group is eating lunch; but even then, I foresee a hill of uneasy possibilities looming over this event. The lunch date is at a semi-fast food restaurant. I imagine taking my son there and sitting him with five or so other children, then feeding him highly processed junk food draped with lettuce so that it can be passed off as "healthy." I imagine the rest of the kids with sugary soft drinks in sippy cups and my son with his organic milk carton asking what it is that they are drinking and why his mama won't let him have one. A half an hour later, the sugar hits the kids' systems and they are all getting hyper, tired, and cranky. More behavior to be upset about.

I imagine all this and then ask myself why I'd possibly want to go.

In this same calendar of events is an incentive for moms to bring in new members. If you rope a friend into joining, you get either a check for five bucks or, prize of prizes, gift certificates for free meals at McDonald's. I loathe the idea of taking my son to McDonald's, or any other polyunsaturated heaven. It's more punishment than prize. I'll take the cash.

Maybe I didn't give this club thing a chance. Perhaps they do charity work, petition to replace the cement yard at the elementary school with grass, or are in the process of implementing a bully program. Actually, I know that they do things to benefit the local battered women's shelter, and I saw a blurb in their newsletter about selling books for some kind of charity. They collect and send old holiday card to the kids at St. Jude's Ranch, just like I do. Hey, we have something in common. Maybe they are working towards building an organic co-op. Maybe it's more about recycling and getting political that I give it credit for. Something about it, though, whether it be the timing, the event or the location, keeps me from attending my first-ever meeting. I keep wondering, as the e-mail roster grows, What's the draw? And why don't I want to play?

There is nothing wrong, I suppose, with stay-at-homes moms wanting to be social. But for me, I have found that I do better with the people I meet through circumstance rather than by design, people who I can enjoy simply for who they are, and not for their role in their family. I like people who do tons of reading, who cannot leave a bookstore without a book in hand. I like people who eat healthy foods and put clean living before anything. I also find those who are a bit wild, like my former self, to be very entertaining and comforting. I like people with tattoos, people who build things. I like people who laugh at my jokes, who don't put on airs. I like people who cook, people who bake, people who love food. I like people who are comfortable in their own skin, kids or no kids.

I don't like the idea of scrapbooking. Actually, I hate it. Scrapbooking is probably the activity I dread doing more than anything else in the world, no holds barred. While the idea of setting up a page, artistically, with photos, is really nice, the whole world of scrapbooking (parties, aisles devoted to, programs about) is terrifying. Wouldn't my time be better spent reading, baking with my son, getting my teeth drilled? When I think of mom groups that are not defined by a way of living (holistic, political, environmental), I think scrapbooking. I think craft circles, craft fairs, craft classes. I think of all the little things that I cannot do, and do not wish to learn. I realize that I may sound like a bitter outsider who judges without experience. But I know that I don't feel bitter when I think these things; I feel frightened. I feel like I am getting lost in a lump of maternal clichés. I know that my presence at one of these events would be a disaster—I am horrible at pretending I'm comfortable in situations that I find unsettling. People can read me like a book. If I am comfortable, there's no hiding it, and if I'm not, I can't hide that either. My guess is that if I attended one of these groups, they'd be holding the door for my early departure, with smiles on.

A man who works in the produce department at the King's supermarket just up the hill from my home, someone who I talk to often, once joked after I told him how shopping for dinner items was my social life, "Don't you have friends?"

My response surprised even me. "Yes, but all this getting together and keeping to a schedule is such a pain in the ass. I'd much rather take my day at my own pace and live in the moments along the way."

It's true. The idea of having to be at someone's house at a certain time gives me performance anxiety. It's fun to show up once in a while, but having my presence counted upon on a regular basis is far too stressful. I prefer to see where the day takes me. I know someday that I will look forward to PTA meetings and dinners with the mothers in my community. I love my community, and the women I have met are interesting people who emanate warmth and invitation. My friends are all ages from all walks of life. I like them because of their intrinsic qualities, not their chosen role. I imagine that there are some women in the local moms' groups who I would really like and could be close to. But when I read the calendar of events, loaded with activities that are either too early for my son and me or too harrowing to enjoy, my stomach lurches. For now, I prefer my solitude, my day-to-day moments, and the time I spend with my son.

Vanity

MANY DAYS, I feel so ordinary. I doubt I've always felt this way, and I wonder if it is a new feeling brought on by motherhood. Feeling ordinary isn't so bad; it's a get-lost-in-the-crowd sort of feeling that keeps life on track and allows time to pass smoothly, without disturbance. It's something that stays with me, day in, day out, and mostly keeps me from being vain.

My ordinariness has become recently more defined. I feel like a loafy old lady, sitting in jeans that are a smidge too short to be cool, practical shoes that show my age, and a body that reveals the wear and tear of pregnancy, birth and motherhood. I imagine that strangers see me and say, "Oh, that poor old thing. She is one giant fashion emergency." I feel my skin wrinkling and in need of a steam, my hair desperately attempting to be trendy but falling just a bit short of it. I am almost a woman, almost whole, almost over the edge. But not.

I wonder if motherhood causes me to feel this way, if my body is responding to ten years of monogamy, or if old age is slipping in quietly and putting me in this gentle place of unattractiveness. I don't yet feel ready to relate to the world of old folks, but I realize that I am not getting any younger. I see people my age who are single, without children, and they seem to be living poles apart from me. They have been to all the new restaurants, had drinks at

bars with friends (often), and feel the freedom that I cannot remember. When I see older and more settled people
who have ten years on these younger counterparts, they
seem kind of like me. Do children rush the aging process,
or is the responsibility of being a parent worn on the body?
I enjoy being a mother, and enjoy the company of my son
over all others, so I know that motherhood works for me.
And I cannot imagine what it would feel like to not be a
mother or have the beautiful love from a child who is my
own. Still, I wouldn't mind having the body, style, and
skin of a twenty-year-old. Why can't I have my cake and
eat it too?

I've recently gone out on a quest for the twenty-first
century's fountain of youth. I have been experimenting
with creams and moisturizers to minimize lines and bring
my skin back to the dewy youthfulness of days gone by.
I've gone so far as to spend $125 on two ounces of mois-
turizing repair cream. I also purchased an age-defying hand
cream to prevent age spots and sun damage—I look down
at my pallid hands and notice two stainlike spots near my
knuckle. Giant freckles or age spots? Who can tell? Can I
buy youth?

Without resorting to scary options like Botox, colla-
gen, or plastic surgery, I wonder if it is possible to age
gracefully. I look at Demi Moore, mother of three (and I
think she nursed them all, too), and see a woman who
looks better in her forties than she did in her twenties,
dating a much younger and very sexy Ashton Kutcher. I
wonder if it's the raw food diet she lived on for a spell or
if she has great genetics. It surely can't be from all the cig-
arettes she smokes, and even if she has had extensive work
done, I cannot believe for the life of me that she is actually older than me.

I look at Madonna, the woman I idolized in the late '80s, and see someone who looks her age. Her body—forget her body, she's insanely fit—but her face looks, well, forty-something. I don't know how or why so much as I know it to be true. She has wonderful skin and is seemingly wrinkle-free, yet she looks her age. Is it the sum of all the things she has done, the people whom she has experienced, motherhood that has changed her face?

When I ask people who look good for their age (whatever that means)—what they do to keep looking young or if they ever feel old—most tell me that they don't think about age, that they find it to be irrelevant. But is it? As a mother, I am constantly being forced to focus on the age of my child. I am always asked, "How old is he?" usually followed by, "Are you going to have any more children?" And on the occasion that I answer, "Probably," I am met with, "You should do it soon before you get too old." Exactly how old is too old? To what age are these people are referring? And if age is irrelevant, why is being "too old" a pregnancy concern?

I like to think of myself as a spiritual person. I like to think that people's opinions of me are irrelevant. Yet when it comes to my vanity, these thoughts go right out the window. Am I pretty enough? Too fat? Do I look too made up? Too plain? Old? I wonder how much of this feeling, this insecurity, rubs off on my son. And at the same time, I am thankful that I do not have a daughter who is learning this skin-deep beauty myth from me.

I wonder if other people feel this way, especially other moms. Did the shift from being childless to being a mother impact the way they view themselves? Has the mother part of them changed the woman part of them? For the first two years of my son's life, I was Mama Earth. I wore no makeup, didn't cut my hair and let the gray edge the Nice and Easy golden blonde color out with a slow, forceful push. I wore jeans until the holes in the knees were too huge to stand. I lived in food-stained T-shirts and shabby nursing bras. Underwear and socks needed only be clean to apply. I stopped moisturizing my skin and only washed my hair when it was screaming for shampoo. On some level, I felt free.

Eventually, the mirrors I'd pass and photos I'd see of myself started barking, "Take care of yourself, please!" I reached a point where I could no longer look at myself in a full-length mirror, and started tweezing my brows, dying my hair, and wearing better clothing. But the process was slow, and over the course of a year, I find myself at the other side of the spectrum. I am obsessed with how I look. I won't leave the house without, at the very least, mascara and some eyebrow pencil. In some way, it makes me feel more in control, but in another, it makes me feel as if I am running against time.

When I was a kid, my mother would drive me to school. I had to constantly remind her of the time, because she'd always be putting on makeup while running out the door. I said to her one morning, "Ma, why do you need to put on makeup just to drop me off at school at seven in the morning?" and she responded, "Tiffany, I might see someone." She was not referring to anyone in particular, just someone in general. Another parent, a teacher, a police officer who would pull her over for speeding, perhaps. And I remember thinking, How pathetic. And now, nineteen years later, I completely understand.

And Baby Makes Four

"SO, WHEN'S THE baby due?" This is the phrase I hate to hear more than anything in the world. The question I am asked so often. But there isn't a baby due. People see a woman with a bulging round belly that is disproportionately larger than the rest of her body and assume. You know what they say about assuming.

The fact is that my ass, in keeping with my belly, is large and bulging; but somehow people don't seem to put the two together, think fat, and keep their mouths shut. Instead, they ask when the baby is coming. Idiots. I have thought about having another child. I've thought about it with much hesitation and fear. The last thing I want right now is a baby. Or a pregnancy.

My pregnancy with my son was wonderful, although adjusting to a new life in my belly, and the fact that it was mine to care for, was tough at first. I had to eat lots of protein but avoid cold cuts (listeria), and pack in plenty of leafy green vegetables. It was important that I drink plenty of water and avoid caffeine at all costs. Once I adapted to the diet overhaul, it was smooth sailing. The first trimester left me mildly nauseated and exhausted due to the raging baby hormones that were taking over my body, and I remember coming home from work every day at six o'clock, collapsing on the couch, and just vegging out for the night, using my husband as my butler and all-around errand boy. I was exhausted for those first three months, but then I got my energy back—it was like my baby was saying, Get off your ass, Mama. The remainder of it was a joy. He was an easy baby to carry. I talked to him all the time, and the minute I found out he was a boy, began calling him by name. However, while my labor, over twenty-six hours of Bradley positions and relaxation techniques followed by two hours of pushing, brought me a most beautiful child, I am in no hurry to relive it. But most importantly, I do not want to disturb the groove we have right now.

We enjoy our time together. There is the occasional tantrum from either John Henry or me, but all considered, we have a blast. We get to do pretty much whatever we want so long as the refrigerator is stocked, the house is livable, and food is on the table sometime between 5:30 and 8 p.m. Our routine is smooth and I'm not yet ready to throw a wrench into the mix. It's like being in high school again, waking up late and forgetting to make the bed, picking our way through half-eaten YoBabys and vines of grapes without a care in the world. As long as we're both clean, showered, and healthy, we can pretty much kick up dust all day and play with backyard ladybugs. Life is so good.

There are concerns attached to getting pregnant again. John Henry is still nursing, but far less frequently, and I believe that the onset of a pregnancy would thrust him back into nursing all the time, and quite frankly, after nearly three years of nursing, I am ready to move on. I cannot imagine breastfeeding during the first trimester. I know women who have done it and I salute them. I also know my limitations and respect them. I choose to hold John Henry whenever he asks to be held, and opt for a sling over a stroller. I cannot imagine how I could do this if I were pregnant. Most importantly, though, I know that John Henry will be little for only a short while and I want to watch him grow, uninterrupted.

At some point, I would like to have another child. I would like to see John Henry grow up with a sibling in the house, someone to whom he could complain about his parents. Someone who would understand. I would like him to have someone to grow up with because I have a brother and he is a real treasure. While we didn't always get along swimmingly, Justin and I always knew that when push came to shove—and often it did—we had each other.

I would like John Henry to have a sibling to help him saddle the burden of caring for his aging parents, if it comes to that. I don't want him to have to do this alone. There is no guarantee that his sibling will help him, or that he will take on the responsibility, or even that we will be fortunate enough to actually age, but it's fair to give him a running chance of having some assistance.

My fear is that, by bringing another human being into the family, I will be hurting my son. How must it feel to see your mama loving another baby in the manner that she loves you, nursing another baby at the breasts that once nourished you, hearing her coo, "I love you," to another child? Even if I were to reassure him by saying, "I love you," to him while I hold or nurse the other child, how would he know I was sincere? I once read that the best way for a mother to imagine how a child would feel would be to imagine if her husband came home with a new, younger wife. If he said he brought her home for me, to bring me company, to help me do the laundry and cook dinner, would it make it easier to watch them kiss? Even if he held my hand and told me he loved me the whole time?

I realize that the relationship a mother and child share is far different from that of a husband and wife, but the jealousy can be just as real. When my brother was brought into this world, five and a half years after I was born, a green monster came alive inside of me. My mother was kept for ten days in the hospital following her cesarean section, and kids were not allowed to visit. I have been told that my dad snuck me in, but I don't remember much about that. I remember feeling abandoned. So when my mom came home ogling a new child, her child, I felt bereft.

A couple of months ago, we decided to adopt a cat. We took John Henry to the shelter and he spotted a beautiful gray cat with a delightful temperament. He sat petting it and said he liked it, that he wanted to take it home. So we brought it home and named it Buster. Within two hours of having Buster in our home, John Henry wanted him out. He hated that the cat was getting all of the attention. At one point, I picked the cat out of a corner where he was sitting uncertainly. I said, "Mama's here, baby," to the cat. John Henry's reply was swift and direct: "He's not baby, I am!" My brother and his girlfriend took the cat into their home the very next day. We probably could have kept it. I'm sure John Henry would have adjusted eventually. But I know the feeling of being displaced all too well, and I didn't think that the cat was worth the pain he would have caused my son.

I realize that someday, should we actually have a baby, the adjustment will be difficult. I believe, though, that the more solid his beginning, the more confident he will be that things will turn out all right. On some level, I am terrified. I am already mourning the loss of our Life of Reilly. But at times I think about John Henry, sitting alone in our house in a snowstorm, wishing he had a playmate, perhaps brother or sister to help him pass the time. I will never know if I have made the right decision, when I make it or when nature makes it for me. How do we ever know how our decisions will affect our children until we do it? I look at John Henry and I think to myself, Don't ruin this beautiful person. But the process of "ruining" someone is not so formulaic, and no one can say for sure what effect big-brotherhood will have on him—or only-childhood, for that matter.

For now, I am not pregnant and we are happy as a party of three. Someday, I hope to find a spark, something to help me decide whether or not another child is in the cards for us. Maybe I'll wake up one day and I'll just decide, and that will be that. Or maybe John Henry will ask for a baby after seeing that his friends have them. When I see kids with their siblings, coexisting happily together, taking care of each other, I want that for my son. I want him to feel closeness and share experiences with a sibling.

Maybe you never feel ready. I mean, who is ever ready for the changes that rock your little snowglobe when a whole new human being enters it?

Full Circle

A S A CHILD, I looked forward to visits at my grandparents' houses. It surely wasn't their actual abodes that excited me—my paternal grandparents lived in a one-bedroom apartment and my maternal grandparents lived in an unruly Cape Cod. Both, however, offered one thing: fun.

I remember that while visiting my Granny and Papa Dave, I would get to play cards all day with Granny, sip on ice cream sodas (that I'd only ever had at her house), and watch her cook. Often Papa Dave was quiet, engrossed in watching the Mets play ball on a squat black and white television. The house would have the heady smell of a Jewish meal, one that began cooking early in the day and would be ready in time for dinner. Granny was raised Southern Baptist, a good Christian girl from Virginia, but her marriage to Papa Dave, a Brooklyn Jew, converted more than just her religion; it converted her cooking. She became a Jewish cook to rival all others. Lucky me. Granny's apartment was right near the beach, in Long Beach, Long Island, yet for some reason, I don't remember that being a draw. I was more excited about helping her place gumdrops, ever so gently, onto her homemade gingerbread house and later, once the house was finished, begging her to let me have a piece to eat.

At Nana and Papa's house, things were different. Inside, I'd help Nana wash and dry dishes (I loved it then) or play on the floor, which tended to always be slightly sticky, as she cooked. She had a dishwasher in her home, but one day, long before I can remember, it broke down and she and Papa just decided to let it be. They began using it for storage and went back to dipping food-caked dishes in soapy water. I can still smell the aroma of the house, a warm smell of food and old linoleum.

The door from their kitchen opened onto a small cement patio covered with a hard plastic awning. The patio spilled out into the yard, forming a half circle enclosed by hedges. From the awning hung lanterns suspended by wires, and both the awning and lanterns were spotted with age. They were like magic to me. This was my stage, the space I used to sing and dance for an imaginary audience and an occasional peeking eye. Beside the house was an old weeping willow. Its lonely branches hung and swayed, beckoning me to come and play. I would swing on them until they could no longer hold me, and then gladly returned to its trunk to rest in its shade.

With all of this, I mostly remember wanting to visit my grandparents because of the way that they loved me. Big arms wrapped around me, soft and stretched with love. I was a golden child to them, my long blonde locks shiny after too many strokes of the brush, blue eyes wide with anticipation of what might be. I ran without worry and rested only when my legs could no longer carry me.

※

My son is already enjoying the free reign he has over my parents' home. When he hears that we are going to Nana's house, he smiles a creeping smile and his eyes roll up and to the right. He is thinking. He begins asking me if he can do all the things that he knows he can do at her house.

"Mama, we go to Nana's house and we gonna go on da slide?" followed by, "And we gonna play with Zadie's nightcrackas?"

I know that going to my mom's house requires an entire afternoon. John Henry will not visit for just an hour—that is when he just begins to settle in. I must wait for two or three hours before beginning to remind him why we must leave. I tell him that we need to go home so Mommy can cook dinner and so that we can see Daddy. Sometimes that's enough. Other times, more prodding is required.

Take for example our Sunday ritual. Sunday is the day we gather as a family at my parents' home. When football is not in season, we usually go for dinner at five and leave by nine. But when football is in season, my husband stays home to watch football games via a dish on a tripod on our roof, unsightly but useful. He is very interested in watching these games and can be very, very vocal (think: expletives and foot stomping). Most often, he will miss the one o'clock games and spend the first part of the day with us. Then, somewhere around three-thirty, as the four o'clock game heads to the airwaves, John Henry and I go to Nana's house. It's good for Johnny because it gives him time to enjoy the game without censor, and nice for us because we get to spend time in a warm, welcoming house filled with delectable foods, fruits, and drinks. As you can guess, I enjoy visiting Nana's house, too.

Today, we started our visit with a Christmas whirl. My mother bought a mini Christmas tree for John Henry to decorate and offered him the finest box of old ornaments a person could imagine. He was in hog heaven as he began to load up the tree with ornaments, one by one, from past Christmases. He hung them on the tree, first all on one side, then the other. My mother sat chuckling as he told her the details of each ornament before he put them on the tree, in the manner that a professor would break down a line of poetry to a class of freshman.

My father, whom John Henry calls Zadie (Hebrew for grandfather, I believe), had returned from a business trip to Texas and had stopped at work to see what had been done while he was away. My mother was anxious for him to see John Henry's tree. She called him at work and requested that he please come home soon: "Saul, you have to come home soon to see the tree John Henry decorated. It's gorgeous." After some time, the door opened. My brother had come for dinner, too, and John Henry was happy to see him. I told him to show Uncle Justin the tree and, when I glanced in its direction, I noticed it was bare. In minutes, John Henry had stripped the tree of all its trimmings.

"Uncle Justin, quick! Help John Henry put the orna-ments on the tree before Zadie gets home," I begged. And while Uncle Justin tried to play along, John Henry decid-ed that he wanted to tackle Justin, the bear. He ran at him and smashed body to body, barely budging my brother. Justin performed a stage fall accompanied by, "Oh, you got me," which only made John Henry want to do it again. This continued for five long minutes and, during all the ruckus, the door creaked open and Zadie walked in.

"Hi, Zadie," I said from a seated position in my moth-er's glider, aware that it might call John Henry to atten-tion. He was up and running. He raced to my father, who looked tired in his jeans and sweater after a long flight, and power-hugged his leg, bestowing it with kisses.

Moments later, he released himself and returned to tackling his uncle.

Over the next three hours, he ate dinner, played more tackle football with his uncle, played Tony the Builder with Nana, jumped in the Jump-O-Lene while we all looked on, saying, "Zadie, look! I fall like dis...," and cuddled in the guest room bed with both Nana and Zadie for a good minute and a half.

It seems that leaving, returning home, had never occurred to him. So, when I mentioned that it was time to go home, he protested.

"I can't wanna go home. I wanna stay here."

I reasoned, "But John Henry, Daddy is waiting."

He huffed, "We see Dada later."

When I asked if he wanted to sleep at Nana and Zadie's house, he responded, "Yes, Mama and John Henry sleep here."

I was up to my ears in trouble.

How does one pull a child out of Wonderland? How could I convince him that it behooved him to put on his sneakers, hat, and coat, to leave this soft, warm spot for a ride in a cold truck to go home and sleep. The only way to convince him that there was a pot of gold on the other side of the rainbow was to give him a peek. So I placed a call to his Daddy, who was at home waiting for us. Daddy is all fun and John Henry enjoys spending time with him as much as he likes being at Nana's. I got Johnny on the horn and asked him to please invite John Henry home. He did so, and John Henry replied, "Okay, maybe later. Okay Dada?" and hung up the phone.

In theory, I could just have forced him to leave. Many people advocate it, explaining that kids need to "know their place." While I understand this position, I do not usually agree with it. My son's place in our lives is in our hearts. He is a sparkling child who will hug me when I cry, hold my chin when he thinks I'm being sweet and say, "Awww," and, when I am exhausted and looking like I was hit by a freight train, he'll say, "Mama, you look booo-tiful." Demanding that he leave without at least trying something more creative was out of the question.

After much discussion and with the promise of a return visit "a morrow," John Henry packed himself up and willingly went to our truck. He climbed into his car seat, satisfied with his visit to his grandparents' house and looking forward to his next visit.

❦

Visits with my grandparents today are far less frequent than they were when I was a child. I have lost both of my paternal grandparents to disease. Papa Dave spent his last days in a hospice after years and years of heart attacks, quadruple bypass surgery, and colon cancer. Granny's death was a painfully slow eight months during which emphysema stole her breath one a bit at a time. I still have my maternal grandparents, both of whom now creak when they stand and require more time getting to the phone, but still have the gusto for keeping company with their granddaughter and great-grandson. I visit them now in the condominium they bought just down the road shortly after we left Long Island for New Jersey. The visits are different for me and far less frequent. I look at them and worry about their health, and think about all the things I should be doing while I'm visiting with them. I reminisce about the old days and try really hard to let them know how they shaped my life. I want them to be sure that they know how very much they mean to me.

I wonder about John Henry, whose grandparents are still young and active. I wonder if, when he is thirty-four, he will still wish to be with them. I wonder if he will find reasons not to visit, forget to call and see how they are doing. I wonder if the guilt of not doing more, not being there for them in their time of need, especially after remembering all they gave to him, will eat him up but still not push him to change.

I like to watch my grandparents interact with my son. As a teenager, I had hoped that they'd all be able to see me get married. Papa Dave was long gone, Granny was in the hospital, but Nana and Papa made it and Papa even sang a song with his twin brothers, accompanied by a harpist, as I walked up the aisle a married woman. I wanted them all to see my child. Nana and Papa have been able to not only see him but know him. Nana laughs at his silliness and bursts with excitement at his every move. He is her fountain of youth. Papa Nick had a rough start with him, two babies both vying for attention, but when they both found their way and Papa grew to understand that John Henry was the one who was a child, they began to form a friendship.

Now, on the rare occasion that we visit them on their turf (usually, we are all at my parents' for Sunday dinner), John Henry explores their house the way I once did when I was young—a newer home but the same old treasures. He is given everything he desires and gets to bang away on Papa Nick's precious baby grand piano, something I am still not permitted to do.

Rocking

FEW THINGS ARE sweeter than the smell of summer. When spring breaks through the walls of snow that the snowplows have built over the course of four months, the ground is moist and buds are just beginning to show. But by the time summer rolls out at the end of June, everything is lush. Trees are packed with leaves and flowers sprout endless blossoms. Ferns are reborn and everything seems so green. This is my time of the year. I like not having to pile on clothes just to get the mail. I like going barefoot, and the warm ground feels so good beneath my feet that the grass stains on them don't go away until fall. It's a time for barbequing and eating outside, and for my son, it means freedom to run everywhere all but naked.

He likes mowing the lawn with his plastic lawnmower from Mumzie that, without the help of batteries, replicates the sound of a real one. He pretends that he's Dada and mows the same patch of lawn until I ask him to switch spots. Other times, he'll pretend he's a builder and will repair our concrete steps with a toy hammer. Or he'll climb the outside of the steps to get the mail. When he can, he throws food to the chipmunk that lives under our porch or the squirrels that chase one another from one tall pine tree to the next.

Here's my joy: rocking in our rocking chairs. When we bought our house, the previous owner left behind two rocking chairs. One was in good shape, and the seat of the other was split. When it became apparent at the end of our first year that we loved rocking on the porch, we decided to get better chairs. We ended up with one adult-sized single rocker, one child-sized rocker, and one two-seater, all from Cracker Barrel. After two years, the weather wreaked havoc on them; in a few more years, these too will need to be replaced.

Our rocking chairs are the most heavily used furniture in our home. As soon as the weather permits, we are outside on those chairs. We sit and rock in them while John Henry plays on the porch, or while we eat pizza. We rock in them on weekend mornings, sipping coffee and watching our neighbors work in their yards. Suzanne pulls up weeds while Rob checks on his growing vegetables. We have deep, meaningful talks with friends on those chairs. Somehow, the rocking soothes people into a safe place, and all their troubles come spilling out and roll away.

I usually go to our favorite garden center, Condurso's, to buy three abundant ferns to hang from the arches of the porch. They act as privacy shields. We can still see everyone who passes—important, because my son and I are big-time wavers—while still feeling like we are in a secret place. Our friend Walter, an ex-NYPD who married a former nun, has a booming voice and a gift for fleshing out old police stories. He always drives by, gives a honk-honk of his horn, and yells out, "Hey, Tiffany!" as if I were the queen of the world. We used to put our ficus tree in the corner of the porch the moment it got warm enough, but when the ficus began to drop leaves, we packed it off for a more suitable home.

My son enjoys his porch time and has spent two summers rocking in his very own rocking chair. Before that, during his first summer, I would sit and rock on the porch, overtired and desperate for a break, while my neighbor and friend, Bambi, held John Henry for hours on end as he jumped and bounced on her lap. Occasionally, we would hear ramblings of a guitar and wonder if we were going crazy. After a moment or two, we would place the music as coming from neighbor Bob, who was plucking away at some strings in the third-floor studio of his Victorian.

Nowadays, having all this neighborly communication is a slice of heaven. I wasn't raised in a house with a porch. My first ten years were spent in a split level on Long Island with a handful of front steps and a fenced-in yard. The neighborhood was fun, full of kids and very little traffic, so despite the lack of porch, I learned to enjoy spending days outdoors. But then, when we moved to a small, isolating cul-de-sac in New Jersey, I found that I needed time to adjust to the new, grand house, set back from the street off of a sloping hill. There were kids out, but we never saw much of our adult neighbors. Everyone spent time in their backyards, alone. They were polite and neighborly, but also very different from the Long Island families. We didn't go for walks or see neighbors passing with their dogs on leashes. The dogs all used their backyards.

I am raising my son in an exceptionally friendly town. People walk their many dogs according to dependable schedules—Jen with Hoagie at 11 a.m., Rita and Joey with Whiskey at 3 p.m.—and I see the same people day after day at approximately the same time. While on maternity leave from my job, at eight months pregnant in a dreary December, I would sit miserably inside and wait for something to happen. Every day at four o'clock on the nose, a man named Tom would walk his dog, Jack, past my house. He was a constant and always looked satisfied with his life. In the years since, I have gotten to know Tom and his wife, Pat, who live two blocks away. We attended their granddaughter Anna's baptism, saw their beautiful daughter Elizabeth as a new mom, and have grown to be close friends. I am rich with the joys of a quiet, tree-lined street packed with neighbors who enjoy living. My son has met more quality people in his first three years of life than I had done in twenty years. We take our water and fruit out onto the porch during what the rest of the world calls rush hour, and we wave to the people driving home from work. What a life.

Lucky

PEOPLE OFTEN WONDER about my family. My mother is normally at my home or otherwise in the company of my son and me at least four days a week. She attends music classes with us, parties, and other sorts of social gatherings. For a long time, she did our food shopping, first for us and later with us. Now, she runs errands with us and visits our home often to play and just be. When John Henry and I get invited to parties, so does my mom. It's almost like we're a set. People will ask me if I know how lucky I am to have my mother around, and a few find it odd. They ask if my mother has nothing better to do, or if her presence is smothering. The answers, of course, vary depending on the day, but all in all I believe that having her in our lives is a blessing.

My son looks forward to seeing her, and on the days we don't see her, he invokes her. He'll see a white vehicle and think it's hers. "Look Mama! That's Nana's car!" Or he will hear a horn beep as it passes the house, look a bit startled, then ask, "Mama, Nana's here?"

I always had my grandparents in my life, perhaps not to this extreme, but I saw them more frequently than most of my friends saw theirs. My friends' grandparents always seemed like the old folks to whom you offer up your cheek for the enforced kiss, then go running to the bathroom to wash off the wetness their lips have left behind. My grandparents, however, were always very cool. They dressed like hipsters and played like children. Granny, my paternal grandmother, wore the funkiest prescription glasses ever. They were made with a pearlized grayish-blue frame shaped like cat eyes and set with rhinestones in the outside corners. Very Bewitched. I always wanted a pair.

My grandparents would roll on the grass with me, play hours of board games and hands of cards, and dance in the kitchen while reheating leftovers. They were the only people who ever babysat me as a child, and when they did, we'd watch The Love Boat and Fantasy Island and have a party. Chips and dips parties, I used to call them. Who the dips were is anyone's guess. They joined all our family vacations, and were always present when I needed an open heart or a shoulder to moisten with tears. The minute there was a problem in our happy little household, I'd call my Nana crying. Before I could even explain, she'd soothe me with kind words and promises of happier times. I am happy that my son shares the same closeness with my mother. Her presence feels right, even when some peoples' sarcastic comments or belittling responses have caused me to question our whole way of relating.

For my most recent birthday, my parents took me to dinner at an intimate family restaurant on the edge of their town, the Columbia Inn. I had been there once before, years ago, and it had not made an impression on me. Once, my husband and I ordered a brick-oven pizza from the place, and although it was excellent, it was very, very small and nearly fifteen dollars. But the restaurant was close enough that John Henry would not fall asleep to a late nap on the way home, so we agreed to go.

As we pulled into the parking lot, I saw my mother go flying out onto Route 202, the two-lane highway in front of the restaurant. I tried honking and high beaming her to no avail. When I was a kid, people would tell me that they saw my mother driving by while they were walking home from school or getting a slice or pizza or something banal. They'd always add how she was busy singing or reapplying her eyeliner. So the fact that she missed the flashing lights and beeping didn't surprise me. I called her on her cell phone to see where the heck she was going, and she told me that she'd forgotten some pom-poms for the table. (I thought pom-pom flowers, but they were, in fact, cheer-leader pom-poms. An unwelcoming flashback of being the only unpopular cheerleader on the whole high school squad tried to distract me from my birthday bliss, but I wouldn't allow it in.) She asked that I go into the restau-rant and wait with my brother and his girlfriend, and told me that the waitress was very nice and had told her that it was fine for her to go get the pom-poms.

We went inside, confused about the pom-poms (what was the big deal anyway?) and an older lady pointed us in the direction of our table. "How do you know who we are?" I asked. She responded by telling me about my mom going home and on and on. I had brought a card and arrangement of flowers, and when the lady (who turned out to be Judy, our waitress) asked who they were for, I told her I wanted to thank my parents for bringing me into the world and continuing to support me throughout my life. I'm a big believer in thanking the people who got me to where I am today, because I'd be nowhere without them. She was thrilled. She told me that she, too, shared a similar relationship with her two adult children. She said she talks to them almost every day (her daughter lives out-side Boston and her son, whose wife was five months preg-nant with twins, lived in Las Vegas) and that their rela-tionship had always been a close one.

"Do you know how lucky you are? That most people don't have this kind of relationship? You know, most people don't even know it exists," whispered Judy into my ear. "Our family still has a big family vacation each year and in June, my husband and I are moving to Las Vegas to be with our son. Our family is everything to us. Other people, people who don't have it…they don't get it. They don't get the whole closeness thing. You're very lucky, you know."

I knew. I thought about it and I realized that Judy was right. So often, people are raised in families where they are not loved, or perhaps they are loved but only from a distance. They become so independent that they cannot separate the joy of sharing time from dependency. They want to teach their children that life is tough and, to prepare them for life, they push them away. Unfortunately, that's not how love works. In my family, we were handled with great love and respect, while still being allowed to explore. At times, the leash may have been a little tight—sometimes enough to strangle—but I always knew that someone wanted to know where I was, someone was waiting home worried. I was able to push back, to fight the curfews and bend the rules. I was able to rebel because there was something to rebel against. I had boundaries and it was up to me to decide how far outside of them I was going to go. Mostly, I knew I was loved, and I knew that a little teen angst would not make that love go away.

My son is surrounded by people who adore him. He functions well in our close-knit circle of comfort. He has never known abandonment or fear in the way that many children have. He enjoys spending time with me and his Dada, Nana and his Zadie, his uncles and aunt, and my mother-in-law, who he calls Mumzie. He has his favorites outside of our family, but mostly he spends time with us.

He is learning our ethics, watching us interact, and learn-ing what it is that we view as right and wrong. In a few years, when he marches off to kindergarten, he will go with a sense of who he is and what he believes in. And when he does, he will leave behind a teary pack of family who feels lucky to have him.

Sleeping Baby

M Y BROTHER TELLS me that my son is not a baby anymore. That, being just shy of three, he is a boy. I disagree. I believe that I will always view my son as a baby probably until the day I die.

❦

Watching someone sleep is incredible. A thousand thoughts rush through my mind like rapids, and all are washed away by the vision before me. When we were first dating nearly ten years ago, I would sit and watch my husband sleep, breathing in his every exhale. I was intoxicated with new love. The same holds true for my son—the intoxication of love, that is. Everything he does overtakes my heart. Smelling his sweet breath, a combination of sourdough and innocence, completely absorbs me. Watching his eyes flutter as dreams play in his mind like movies reminds me how very thin his peaceful eyelids are.

I enjoy watching his breath fill his belly to a taut expansion and then, very slowly, release through his full, soft lips. I think about the fact that his breath is his life and I am thankful for every bit of air that he breathes. I watch his hand, fingers still chubby, curl in a sweet position on the bed. His index finger moves, as if he is talking with his hands in his dream but only has the physical energy to move a finger in sleep. Occasionally I will be surprised by a word or two that slips off his tongue, the hint of a dream that he will not remember or share with me. It's as if I get to glimpse into his unconscious, if only for a second.

I cannot imagine him sleeping anywhere else but where he is, in our room, in our bed. I would not be at the receiving end of 4 a.m. kicks, but I would miss the soft cuddles into my back or the hand that fortuitously falls into mine. I would never know that he wakes once or twice during the night, sits up and looks around, and then lies down again, returning to sleep as if he'd never left it.

I wonder if I'll someday want to reclaim that space in the middle of the bed. Right now, it is unimaginable. I'd rather sleep on the floor to allow him more room than push him to sleep alone. I do not wish to lose this precious time. Sometimes, I'll snuggle my head near enough to his heart just to listen to it beat. The rhythm is a stunningly serene boom that brings me straight to God.

A couple of months ago, John Henry woke from a long nap. It was to be one of his last for a while, but at the time I didn't know it. He looked at me and asked me to get his "Cookie Puppet." When I returned with the puppet in hand, on hand, he asked, "Cookie Puppet, do you believe in angels?"

I tried, as Cookie Puppet, to decipher the meaning of this question. Was it really that simple? Did my son, who has not been exposed to any sort of organized religion or talk of angels, really want to know if I, or Cookie Puppet, or someone believed in angels? I asked him if he'd dreamt about angels and he said yes. When I asked what they looked like, he told me that they had blue hats, and then got on the floor and pulled out a wooden nativity that I bought him the Christmas prior. Inside, he pointed to one of the wise men and said, "See the angel?"

❦

My son is, at this moment, sleeping beside his father in a bed less than twenty feet from me but a wall apart. Occasionally he sighs and I jump up to see if he is about to awaken. If I am not in bed when he wakes, he will try and find me, which will jar him into a state of unrest. You see, because he is a baby, he still needs the warmth and reassurance of a parent through the night—not unlike adults, who tend to like to share their beds with partners. I know that I never enjoyed sleeping alone. I relished sleepovers with friends, and between the time when sleepovers ended and marriage began, I was terrified of sleep. I'd stay up until 3 or 4 a.m., and only then, lights bright and television blaring, would I be able to fall asleep. Perhaps it is because as a baby I didn't have a chance at a family bed. Who knows?

It is late and I am going to my bedroom to sleep. I will watch my son breathe. I will look at him, just more than half my length, and wonder how he ever fit inside my body. How did he start so very, very small and then grow to the size of a peach pit, then an apple, a melon, and finally so large that my body would no longer accommodate him? And how has he grown from there? How has he come to be a boy who talks, dresses himself, and runs around so quickly?

I see how very tender he is, how gentle and small with needs so great and thin, pale flesh, and I will remember that he is my baby, always.

John Henry

THE DAY I came home with my son, John Henry, I sat with him in my arms, staring at the nine-pound bundle with a single hank of hair and wondered how people put babies down. When he wasn't nursing, he was sleeping. I could not bring myself to abandon him to his bassinet. I worried that he would get cold or that the space would feel too vast for him. After being in the womb for forty weeks, the only place for him, I believed, was in my arms. I sat in a big plaid reading chair with my knees up to my chest, cradling my son atop them in my arms. Looking at this sheer miracle, this big soul in such a delicate body, brought me to tears. I looked up at my mother, who was sitting across from me, and I said, "Mom, how am I going to leave him to go to work?" She looked at me knowingly and said, "Daddy never expected you to go back to work. He wouldn't want you to."

I am fortunate to have parents who put family first. My father helped to take care of us whenever necessary because he believed that it was important for me to be at home with John Henry. I don't know how I would have done it if the situation had been different. How could I have left him?

In those first months, my mother arrived at my home somewhere between eight and nine in the morning. She would make me breakfast, do the laundry, and clean the

house. She would hold John Henry for me while I showered or rested. She did all my grocery shopping and always
made dinner. During snowstorms, she would ask my father
to drive her to my house. If the roads weren't too bad,
she'd go it alone. She went to all of my appointments with
me—to see my midwife or my son's pediatrician—and sac-
rificed everything to be with us.

Being at home was scary at first. I don't know what
scared me, though. Perhaps it was the huge responsibility
of caring for another human being. I frequently checked to
see if he was breathing, something I've learned is common
among new mamas. At night, he slept on my chest, making it easy to monitor his vitals. My body temperature reg-
ulated his so that he was never too cold or too warm. He
was always snug on mama's big mound of breasts.

As he got older, much of the routine changed. But
even now, I cannot imagine going to work without him. If
I needed to work, I'd find a job that allowed me to bring
him along. I know many intelligent, educated women who
have decided to stay home and sacrifice amenities. These
women are my role models because understand the gravi-
ty of being a mother, and they take their "jobs" very seriously.

Tonight I was telling my son about the things we did
he was little (heck, he's only two, but to him, baby means
little). I tell him of the days that I spent staring dreamily
into his eyes, in complete awe of the grace God had given
me. I tell him how I used to dance him to sleep in the sling
while listening to Kenny Loggin's Return to Pooh Corner.
I show him how I caressed his face with my finger, petted
his head with a gentle hand, and let him know how much
I loved him by telling him over and over again.

You know what he said to me? He said, "Mama, know
why I love you? I love you eyes, you nose, you heya (hair),

you mauf (mouth), you eais (ears), you nose, you whole fing."

It doesn't get any better than this.

Acknowledgements

T HERE ARE MANY people whom I wish to thank, and do so here in no particular order. Wherever you are on this list, know that you are top-rate in my eyes.

To my son, John Henry, who is everything to me; my sweet, wonderful, understanding, supportive husband, Johnny; my mom and dad; Nana, Papa Nick, Justin, Colleen, Granny, and Papa Dave, you are my family. Laura Caravano Hall, my dear friend and shepherd in the stay-at-home world, you are my lifeline. Thank you for your precious and generous laugh. To Heather, J. J., Jay, and Mumzie, thank you for treating me like I'm blood, and for knowing me and still loving me. To Dr. Rob Gilbert, the person who taught me that I could always follow my dreams and that writing a book starts one page at a time. To my unexpected wonderfuls, all of you, but especially Rob Welz, Mike Sullivan, Jim Miller, John Stahl, Leigh from Heavenly Temptations, Donna Baccaro, Vicki and Rob Cobane, Anne Bourault, Tom and Pat Walsh, Walter and Pat Krebs, Jennifer Coultas, Suzanne Farese and Bob "Mickey" Spillane (of WNTI radio), Chris and Dan Bailey, the Dalrymples, Karen DeMas, Lynn and Roberta (for the chocolate treats for John Henry) from Gri Gris, Michelle at the LH post office; and Kim, Sean, Sue and Joe Flatt, Kathy, Nina, Steve, Louis, Bill, and Gail from King's, and everyone at Condurso's. You all make my world a brighter place. To Meredith Hayes, Sarah Cypher, Kristin Johnson, and Susan Wenger, for turning my rough essays into this beautiful little thing. To Sharon Lewis, Bob Whitney, and Eliot Graff, the people who made studying English an unforgettable experience. You sing in my heart. And to Anthony Amoroso, Lisa Cunningham, and Diana Paiotti who helped get me through being a full-time student while holding a full-time job—we actually did it. To all of my wonderful friends and their children, especially Jenifer and James O'Neill and Janet, Hannah, and Elias Winters, who I don't see enough and love with all my heart. Thank you for being there and for helping me understand the task of both a mother and a woman. And to our favorite places, especially our Wednesday places (you know who you are). Thanks for letting us live our world in the safety of your warm, inviting spaces.

Printed in the United States
23599LVS00001B/481-486

9 781587 362293